Jonathan Keates

—

THE PORTABLE PARADISE

Baedeker, Murray, and the Victorian Guidebook

—

Notting Hill Editions

Published in 2011
by Notting Hill Editions Ltd
Newcombe House, 45 Notting Hill Gate
London W11 3LQ

Designed by Flok, Berlin, Germany
Typeset by CB editions

Printed and bound
by Memminger MedienCentrum, Memmingen, Germany

A CIP record for this book
is available from the British Library
ISBN 978-1-907-90302-1

www.nottinghilleditions.com

— THE PORTABLE PARADISE —

I can't honestly remember how I began collecting guidebooks. It had something to do, maybe, with an enormous novel, forever in progress, which I wrote as an undergraduate. Set in France, Germany and Italy in the years immediately before 1914, this interminable work, to which I subjected my long-suffering friends, was provisionally entitled *The Marquis, or They Are Not to be Had on the Spot*. The subtitle – chosen out of sheer cussedness, I now have to confess – came from the opening pages of Murray's *Knapsack Guide To Norway* (1869).

In quest of local colour for my narrative I had found myself ransacking Murray, Baedeker and other travel books of the pre-First World War period. My novel may have gone the way of all fictional flesh, but an addiction was born. I soon learned that the name Baedeker should be pronounced not 'Bydeker' or 'Beadeker', but 'Baydeker', the 'ae' being merely a phonetic rendering of the original German 'ä'. Over the years my collection of such volumes grew organically. They now seem to me battered survivors from the days when second-hand bookshops were run by grubby old curmudgeons in carpet slippers, who did not, unlike their modern avatars, hide the antiquarian stock in locked cases, and who priced their books with a thought or two for the interests of dedicated readers.

In those days, no one had much time for an out-of-date guidebook, especially intellectuals, for whom proper history did not take place on the margins or in ephemeral genres. The prejudices of the day were those of George Steiner, who once complained of Jane Austen that 'at the height of political and industrial revolution, in a decade of formidable philosophical activity, Miss Austen composes novels almost extra-territorial to history'. Yet I have always believed that, for all the fact that she does not discuss the causes of the Napoleonic Wars head-on, Austen gives us the texture of life as it was lived during the first two decades of the nineteenth century in a way that is entirely central to history.

Guidebooks may seem at first glance unreliable witnesses to the past. They date so quickly and their information as to the tourist infrastructure of cities and resorts is rendered worse than useless by the rapidity of social and economic change. For similar reasons their illustrations, after a very short while, offer embarrassing reminders of the truth enunciated in one of his short stories by Somerset Maugham that 'No day is so dead as the day before yesterday.' Nothing ever looks quite as sad, in both the traditional and modern senses of that word, as an old guidebook dragged out into the sunlight by a modern traveller.

The truth is, nevertheless, that in the same degree as their usefulness and relevance diminishes, so
the significance of guidebooks from an entirely different perspective grows more substantial. Through
being gradually rendered 'extra-territorial' in the
purely physical sense, they become indispensable
companions to another territory entirely, that
immense, enduringly resonant space created by the
culture and aspirations of an evolving society at a
given stage in its development. After due seasons
of practical use and ensuing neglect, a guidebook
renews its existence as a conspectus of what its
original purchasers (perhaps more important, in
this respect, than its author or publisher) dreamed
of, hankered after and eventually succeeded in discovering. Whether as professional historians or as
everyday readers anxious for a closer walk with the
past, we do wrong in ignoring these books as valid
witnesses of their own era.

These books speak as physical artifacts. None of
the guides in my collection is in mint condition, and
I should be very suspicious if that were the case.
Admittedly, my Baedeker's *Greece* (fourth edition,
1909) has a slight air of never having wandered
much further than the bookshop in the Strand
where it was originally sold at 3/6d, but the others
are battered and dog-eared with the experience of
frequent use and hard travel. Their covers have faded

from the original scarlet to interesting shades of rose madder, salmon pink and terra cotta. The various volumes in the Murray's *Handbook* series have been still more roughly handled. Successive ramblers through Anatolia have placed the 1905 *Asia Minor* almost beyond redemption via the loving attentions of a bookbinder, while the *Portugal* evidently spent so many years under a torrid Lusitanian sun, with accompanying splashes of seawater, that its cockled covers have bleached to an earthy beige. Comparatively few of the Murrays preserve the folding maps originally held in a specially designed wallet inside the book's back board. Here and there, what is more, the traveller has jotted down a little list of expenses, noted the names of hotels not listed in the guide, or added marginal question and exclamation marks beside the author's comments. My copy of the 1913 Baedeker's *Spain and Portugal* belonged to the poet John Masefield, who whiled away an idle Iberian hour by playing a game of telegrams on the fly leaves with his companions. The state of the handwriting suggests that they were on a fast train or a violently rocking ship at the time, and they kept their messages topical – 'Jemima Sailing Aquitania For Los Angeles Or Indies As Last Resort, Alfred,' reads one; 'Maria Has Burned Every Fig Tree, Help! Letitia At Cadiz,' says another.

The archaeology of the guidebook, the sense of it as a place of occupational layers where miscellaneous objects lie scattered in suitably enigmatic confusion, has its own unique poignancy and – to use the word in a continental rather than an English sense – suggestiveness. Which of those trains from Saumur to Angers, whose times he hastily scribbled on the back of a hotel bill tucked into Black's guide to Touraine and Brittany, did R. Hustler of Newton Road, Torquay, finally catch? Who gathered the harebells, meadowsweet and sheepsbit scabius pressed between the pages of Baedeker's *Paris and its Environs*, each marking places so resoundingly urban that the last time a wild flower can have grown there was in the days when Julius Caesar was attacking the Gaulish tribes? As a bookmark for my copy of Appleton's *United States and Canada* someone has used an envelope from one of the state rooms of a transatlantic steamer of the Allen Line out of Liverpool. The envelope was sealed, and I have so far left it unopened.

It's easy to grow sentimental over things like these. Often I like to smell books, and the gamiest of scents float off the pages of an old *Guide Bleu*, a wormy Ward Lock, or a damp-speckled exemplar of the Conti series, which covered the various French *départements* in obsessive detail during the nineteenth century's final decades. A guidebook, by such tokens, becomes a spur to the overactive imagination, and the very name of its publisher, let alone its physical appearance or the litter among its pages, has a talismanic quality, an aura of romance. Our sense of the past, 'without the which we are pictures or mere beasts', is nurtured in a variety of important ways by those very qualities in a guidebook which condemn it to the ultimate indignity of a place in one of those cardboard boxes labelled 'Everything for 50p' which we find on the pavement outside a charity shop. That very same sense of 'the inaudible and noiseless foot of Time' sounding rather more loudly because of the ephemeral nature of these works is precisely what asserts their significance. The fact that in Yokohama we can no longer buy our biscuits and brandy at Lane & Crawford of 59 Main Street, that in Cairo no ladies' orchestra beguiles the patrons of the Café Egyptien (does it still exist? If so, under what name, and were the musicians similar to those whom Joseph Conrad, in *Victory*, immortalizes as 'murdering silence'?), or that in Siena we cannot still hire saddle horses from Ceccarelli in Via Cavour, is each of them a resonant absence worth explaining.

There is, it must be said, a monumentality, a quality almost of the epic, about Baedeker, Murray, their clones and epigones, which absolutely defies us to dismiss them as ephemeral. Though most (if not quite all) of their practical information is no longer useful, the depth of perspective within their coverage of what Shakespeare calls 'the memorials and the things of fame that do renoun this city' (whichever it may be), together with the historical backgrounds they provide, gives each of these books an inalienable seriousness and authority. Such qualities, more especially in the field of art history, are mediated for us by the sense of a rational discourse which never seeks to overpower the reader with the dogma of critical orthodoxy. In each of Murray's handbooks, there is certainly a deliberate attempt made at evolving an aesthetic hierarchy among the noteworthy attractions of a particular town or region, with buildings or paintings starred accordingly. Yet, as with Baedeker, the tyranny of good taste and received wisdom is less important to the writers of these books than the fact that we, the travellers, are out there, on the spot, forming our own opinions, quite often in the teeth of theirs. Even long after their recommendations for hotels and restaurants have become redundant, they still intrigue, infuriate, and invite us to engage.

—

The pre-history of the guidebook, which arose in its modern form during the second decade of the nineteenth century, is not so 'extra-territorial' to the momentous events of history as one might have supposed. In fact, one such historical moment was formative in the development of the guidebook as a literary genre: the English Civil War, taking place during the middle decades of the seventeenth century. As the interests of King Charles I and his

Parliament grew more polarized during the late 1630s, with open conflict between the two sides breaking out in 1642, some younger members of the English gentry made up their minds not to participate directly in the war, whatever their political or religious sympathies. I'm reminded at this point of a neat observation by the lawyer and amateur musician Roger North, who notes of his musically inclined contemporaries at this period that 'many chose rather to fidle at home, than to goe out and be knockt on the head abroad'.

But what of those who preferred to fiddle abroad, metaphorically if not actually, rather than stay at home to be knocked on the head? The era saw a notable increase in the number of travellers slipping out of England to spend long spells wandering through France, Holland, Germany and Italy. John Evelyn, for example, newly graduated from Oxford, occupied almost nine years, between 1641 and 1650, with journeys up and down continental Europe, writing up most of them to create one of the most valuable and entertaining records of travel produced during the seventeenth century. Like many others retreating across the English Channel, he was a Royalist, and his trip, like theirs, may in some sense have represented a self-imposed exile.

In such travels we can see the beginnings of what would later become known as the Grand Tour, an essential element of aristocratic and gentry culture during the following century. Making the journey, these pioneer tourists of the 1640s needed advice on what to see, where to stay, how much money to take, what languages to learn and what – or whom – to avoid. Some of the earliest exemplars of the guidebook as we now know it sprang from imperatives created directly or indirectly by the decisive Parliamentarian victories at Marston Moor and Naseby, by the various attempts on the part of Parliament itself to institutionalize puritan worship in place of the suspect Popery represented by Laudian Anglicanism, and by the eventual arrest, trial and execution of King Charles I.

In 1642, the very year when the armed struggle commenced, the Welsh writer James Howell, a committed Royalist, produced his *Instructions for Forreine Travell*. His previous book, and the one for which he became best known, *Familiar Letters or Epistolae Ho-Elianae* (1641) – the title incorporates a Latin version of his surname – is dedicated to the King as 'the centre of our happiness'. In an introductory poem entitled 'The Vote, or a Poem-Royal', Howell boasts that:

I have had audience (in another strain)
Of Europe's greatest kings, when German main
And the Cantabrian waves I crossed, I drank
Of Tagus, Seine and sat at Tiber's bank,
Through Scylla and Charybdis I have steered,

Where restless Aetna's belching flames
    appeared,
By Greece, once Pallas garden then I praise't,
Now all o'erspread with ignorance and waste,
Nor hath fair Europe, her vast bounds through-
    out,
An academy of note I found not out.

The correspondence making up *Familiar Letters* stretches over two decades of Howell's peripatetic career. 'In the carriage and course of my rambling life,' he tells the virtuoso Sir Kenelm Digby in the final letter, 'I had occasion to be, as the Dutchman saith, a landloper, and to see much of the world abroad.' There are letters from Alicante, Paris and Hamburg, Bilbao, Naples and Orleans, and there is much practical and political wisdom on Venice, 'still gay, flourishing and fresh, and flowing with all kind of bravery and delight', despite the fact that her economy is in decline, 'since Portugal found a road to the East Indies by the Cape of Good Hope'. There is gossip from the Spanish court (King Philip's chief minister Olivarez watches a nubile infanta 'as a cat doth a mouse'), and details of the current French craze for bloodletting: 'Phlebotomy is so much practised here, that if one's little finger ache, they presently open a vein . . . the commonness of the thing taketh away all fear.'

In an era which saw the earliest incarnations of

the modern newspaper, Howell was a born journalist, with a nose for good copy and the touches essential for making it fly off the page. The same instincts inspired *Instructions for Forreine Travell*. The writer had spotted a niche market in the Royalists hurriedly distancing themselves from the approaching clash of arms on the pretext of a voyage to Italy, several of them, as Papists, genuinely alarmed at the prospect of an abrupt end to the climate of toleration for their faith which had prevailed under an Anglican monarch married to a Catholic princess. The book is not just a compendium of handy information for travellers on the Continent but an encouragement to the English (such as can afford it) to broaden their horizons. 'Amongst other people of the Earth,' says Howell, 'Islanders seeme to stand in most need of Forraine Travell, for they being cut off (as it were) from the rest of the Citizens of the World, have not those obvious accesses & contiguity of situation and other advantages of society, to mingle with those more refined Nations whom Learning and Knowledge did first Urbanize and polish.' It was not simply in the name of sophistication that Englishmen had a duty to travel, according to Howell, but for the sake of their spiritual improvement. The stars and planets, after all, move around the sky and we would do well to imitate these celestial voyages.

An important part of the civilizing process thus envisaged lay in learning foreign languages. The writer of *Instructions for Forreine Travell* was himself a gifted linguist – he later compiled one of the first polyglot dictionaries – but he is at pains to discourage his readers from trying to acquire too authentic and convincing an accent once they grasp the outlines of the tongue in question. English travellers in France, for example, should under no circumstances try 'to speake like naturall Frenchmen, and to get the true genuine tone'. They should try, on the other hand, to make adequate social contact with the natives. 'The greatest bane of English Gentlemen abroad is too much frequency and communication with their own Countrey men.'

More detailed practical advice in Howell's manual includes a recommendation to carry a note-book at all times. 'He must always have a Diary about him, when he is in motion of Journeys, to set down what his Eye meetes with most remarquable in the day time.' Following in his footsteps, I personally carry around with me those small black notebooks marketed as 'the Alwych book with the All-Weather cover'. In them I note everything from quotations, book titles, phone numbers, and email addresses to London restaurants, Parisian hotels, and the large number of churches in Rome I've still not visited. There are occasional accounts of my more bizarre or disturbing dreams; there are pages devoted to early uses of modern-sounding words and expressions ('high flier', 1691; 'kick the bucket', 1781; 'no can do',

1912; etcetera); and there are epitaphs collected from churches ('Her patience was exercised by a variety of afflictions till made meet for glory' says the memorial to poor Sarah Hickinbotham of Ratcliffe-on-Soar, Nottinghamshire; 'He just stop'd here below On his journey to Above And felt ye Agonies of Expiring nature to heighten his Relish of ye Joys of Heaven' runs that of John Paston of Barningham, Norfolk). To lists of odd-sounding names culled from the newspapers – Larisa Trimbobler, Swidbert Ott, Sue Other-Gee, Giles Muddle, Arch Puddington, Natalie Hardbattle – is added a section headed 'Things I've Done Which Embarrass Me' and another entitled 'Bad Lines in Shakespeare'.

Unlike me, Howell's pragmatic touring cavalier in the seventeenth century must have used his notebook – an ancestor of the Alwych, the Moleskine and its various imitators – to jot down a hasty calculation of current expenses. Though he could move freely around Europe with the help of letters of credit and bills of exchange, he needed to keep a sharp eye on the outgoings. In Paris, 'that hudge (though durty) Theater of all Nations', the total cost of a year's stay – including servants at £50, 'Riding, Dancing, Fencing, the Racket [Real Tennis], Coach-hire, with other casuall charges, together with his Apparell' – amounted to an eye-popping £300.

'With the naturall situation of Countreyes,' Howell suggests, 'a Traveller should observe also the Political position thereof.' John Raymond, in his *Il Mercurio Italico* (1648) was evidently of the same mind. This little book is an agreeable mixture of travel narrative, guidebook and vade mecum along Howellian (or Ho-Elian) lines. The would-be voyager, after coping with the 'three evitable dangers that divert some from the voyage', namely the climate, a profusion of bandits, and the notional menace of the Holy Inquisition, could settle down to enjoy such Italian nonesuches as 'that worthy peece of arte the Falling Tower' in Pisa or 'that richest of Treasures, the great Dukes Gallery' at Florence, where the Boboli Gardens displayed 'here a Sea of Fountaines, there Swans, Austriches and other recreative Creatures'. At Siena, the people are 'very courteous, a great deale suiting to the humours of foreigners, and besides the purity of the Italian language is here profest and spoken'. Elsewhere, however, 'the Plebeians or Comonalty of Italy savour much of the Goths and Vandalls', though not so much in Rome or Naples, where Raymond notes 'a residue of the old Genius still surviving' among the citizens.

The *Mercurio* also features one of the earliest indications of what later became a key element in any guidebook, the amount of time needed for sightseeing in a given location. 'Hee that would see Rome may doe it in a fortnight, walking about from Morning to Evening, he that would make it his study to understand it, can hardly perfect it in lesse than a yeare.' Though Raymond does not resort to the star system favoured by modern guide-writers, he has clear priorities for the book's user where the wonders of Rome are concerned. On no account should we miss the Colosseum, the gardens of the Villa Borghese, and such marvels of antique statuary as the Laocoön, the Romulus and Remus, or the Niobe. As for St Peter's Basilica, 'In a word, tis the most perfect model of decent Magnificence in the world.'

As the seventeenth century continued, the whole phenomenon of extended travel through France and Italy (with possible diversions into Germany, Austria and Holland) took on the form we now know as the Grand Tour. Classically this would require an absence from England of at least a year, often more, during which the young and affluent male of noble family journeyed south, spending time in Venice, Florence, Rome, and Naples so as to improve his taste through exposure to the various arts of Italy, sometimes meeting and patronizing the artists themselves. Adequate acquaintance with painting, sculpture, music and the specialized discourse of connoisseurship would ultimately enable him to bring home a collection worthy of the houses he built for himself in town or country to show it off.

The youthful dilettante, whom his English servants addressed as 'm'lord' – soon adopted by Italians as *milord* or *milordo* – was usually accompanied by a tutor specially engaged for the trip. Such figures were sometimes footloose clergymen, dons moonlighting from Oxford and Cambridge, parsons fallen foul of the clerical establishment for their Jacobite politics or their sexual indiscretions, or else they were selected from among the often rather dubious expatriate communities settled in the different art cities en route. Since his lordship was, by inference, unpolished and gross, the guide employed was jocularly dubbed his 'bear-leader', referring to the men who earned a living from the dancing bears they lugged from town to town.

For the greater part of the eighteenth century bear-leaders kicked the guidebook into the long grass. Grand-tourism became an expensive undertaking: the cost of putting a travelling carriage on the road was prohibitive, let alone that of establishing one's status, once arrived in Italy, with the necessary retinue of servants, periodic splashes of hospitality, and the right clothes for a court ball, or an evening at the opera. Sightseeing for the *milordi* was essentially a social exercise, matter for listening and discussion rather than for bite-sized enlightenment from the pages of a book. A not unimportant aspect of the Grand Tour was that only a very few people could actually afford it and bear-leaders did not come cheap.

The guidebook to the Continent in its modern, democratic form was a sort of virtual *cicerone*, a Grand Tour on the cheap. But it did not come into being until after the end of the Napoleonic Wars. By then, social and economic changes were already transforming tourism into a middle-class phenomenon, but as long as the war continued Britons had to make do with the British Isles themselves, until the peace of 1815 sent them scrambling in their thousands to the Channel ports and the Thames estuary for places on the packet boats to Calais, Boulogne, Ostend, and Antwerp. The enforced stay-at-home period, lasting roughly from 1802 to the end of hostilities in 1815, marked a phase of tourism which can be seen as a kind of transitional proving-ground between the leisurely aristocratic progress of the Grand Tour and that omnium-gatherum seasonal exodus to the Continent which created a holiday market for the Victorian bourgeoisie.

During this period the improved British roads pioneered by Telford and Macadam, together with changes in the technology of coach-building – notably the introduction of the inverted C-spring, making the body of the carriage more buoyant in relation to the road surface – meant that tourists could now bowl along more briskly in search of the 'beauties' recommended by Romantic landscape enthusiasts. Thus in *Pride and Prejudice* (1813), Jane Austen places the novel's crucial narrative sequence, at the opening of Volume 3, against the background of a trip to Derbyshire proposed by Elizabeth Bennett's aunt and uncle Gardiner several chapters earlier. 'We have not determined how far it shall carry us,' says Mrs Gardiner, 'but perhaps to the Lakes.' Elizabeth, temporarily alienated from humanity by the silliness of Mr Collins and the hauteur of Mr Darcy, grows almost Wordsworthian in her response. 'My dear, dear aunt, what delight, what felicity! You give me fresh life and vigour. Adieu to disappointment and spleen. What are men to rocks and mountains? Oh! what hours of transport we shall spend!'

Seasoned Austen readers will understand this effusion as a warning signal from the author. Her consistently anti-Romantic ethos invites an immediately raised eyebrow in the direction of any heroine who prefers rocks and mountains to men. But Elizabeth Bennett goes further. 'And when we do return,' she declares, 'it shall not be like other travellers, without being able to give one accurate idea of any thing. We *will* know where we have gone – we *will* recollect what we have seen. Lakes, mountains and rivers shall not be jumbled together in our imaginations; nor, when we attempt to describe any particular scene, will we begin quarrelling about its relative situation. Let *our* first effusions be less insupportable than those of the generality of travellers.'

A guidebook, some might feel, would help in this respect. Not altogether ironically, when the party return from their jaunt to the Peak District, there is hardly a suggestion that its beauties have made any impression on them. Instead, the redemptive process undergone by Darcy and Elizabeth has commenced, its path mapped out with the help of Lydia's dramatic elopement from Brighton with the disreputable Wickham. Nature, instead of being merely a passive recipient of fashionable enthusiasm or even a validator of genuine sensibility, is accorded a far subtler role, among the Pemberley chapters, in the first of those symbolic engagements with landscape through which Austen reveals herself as a genuine innovator among the novelists of her period.

A year after the publication of *Pride and Prejudice* Napoleon was defeated at Leipzig and banished to Elba. The 'Hundred Days' following his escape from the island and reinstatement as emperor were ended by the allied victory at Waterloo. Would Elizabeth and Darcy, now married and installed at Pemberley, have wanted to join in the gleeful scamper to the Continent which followed? Another Jane Austen character, 'the charming Augusta Hawkins' whom Mr Elton brings home to Highbury as his bride in *Emma*, is the sort who would jump at the chance. In a novel which celebrates immobility, one where almost every journey is fraught with some kind of danger, Mrs Elton's inability to sit still is an implicit mark against her, and we can almost feel the authorial shudder when she is overheard, having sent her carriage to bring Jane Fairfax to the ball at the Crown, remarking: 'I believe we drive faster than anybody.' She irritates Emma on their first meeting by her references to 'exploring' in her brother-in-law Mr Suckling's barouche-landau, and it is Mrs Elton who organizes the jaunt to Box Hill which ends in disaster and misery for several of those who choose to join it.

Such fretfulness reflects the restless temper of the age. About ten years after *Emma* was published (in 1815, the very year of Waterloo) Samuel Taylor Coleridge offered his own analysis of the zeitgeist in a piquant, though still seldom read, satirical poem, 'The Delinquent Travellers':

> O, what scores are sick of Home,
> Agog for Paris or for Rome!
> Nay! tho' contented to abide,
> You should prefer your own fireside;
> Yet since grim War has ceased its madding,
> And Peace has set John Bull a-gadding,
> 'Twould such a vulgar taste betray,
> For very shame you must away!

The Mrs Eltons of this world now ruled and tourism in its modern form was rampant.

> Keep moving! Steam, or Gas, or Stage,
> Hold, cabin, steerage, hencoop's cage –
> Tour, Journey, Voyage, Lounge, Ride, Walk,

Skim, Sketch, Excursion, Travel-talk –
For move you must! Tis now the rage,
The law and fashion of the Age.

Such continental drift, a species unknown to geographers, was not just for the sake of movement alone, at least according to Coleridge. His delinquent travellers are those quitting England not through a psychotic reaction to war-induced cabin-fever, but because of a need to clear out before the law takes hold of them.

Rogues, rascals, sharpers, blanks and prizes,
Delinquents of all sorts and sizes,
Fraudulent bankrupts, knights burglarious,
And demireps of means precarious.

Landing at Boulogne, he finds the place already thronged with such low life.

But bless us! what a numerous band
Of cockneys anglicize the strand!
Delinquent bankrupts, leg-bailed debtors,
Some for the news and some for letters –
With hungry look and tarnished dress,
French shrugs and British surliness.

Yet even these are not quite the kind of figure Coleridge is in search of as an alternative to the competitive mob of tourists as fashion-victims castigated earlier in the poem. Out in the waters of the Channel a transport ship heaves into view, carrying convicts to the Antipodes. This is one tour the poet longs to join:

> Of Diemen's Land the elected Gentry,
> And founders of Australian Races –
> The Rogues! I see it in their faces!
> Receive me, Lads! I'll go with you,
> Hunt the black swan and kangaroo.

Coleridge, with that vatic insight granted to his kind since the age of Homer, foresees the way whereby an Australia of the future will transcend its unrespectable past:

> We'll have a virtuous progeny;
> And on the dunghill of our vices
> Raise human pine-apples and spices.

The true delinquents, as Coleridge sees them, are:

> the children of John Bull
> With empty heads and bellies full,
> Who ramble East, West, North and South,
> With leaky purse and open mouth.

It was for this kind of traveller, from whom the poet of 'Kubla Khan' and 'The Rime of the Ancient

Mariner' was so anxious to dissociate himself, that the guidebook in its modern avatar came into being.

—

Karl Baedeker, founder of the German guidebook series, was born in Essen in 1801, the son of a bookseller. The educative aspect, which is such a powerful feature of the guides, derived from Baedeker senior's interest in publishing school texts, how-to manuals, and works of popular science. When Karl started up his own business in the Rhineland town of Coblenz in 1827, he hit on the notion of catering for the local growth industry of tourism on the Rhine itself. Overhauling a guide to the Rhineland by a local professor, he issued his streamlined version in 1836. Subsequent editions were improved with ideas borrowed from the *Handbook For Travellers On The Continent*, which appeared in the same year from the London firm of John Murray, famous as Byron's publisher. The system of organized routes from one town to another, the awarding of stars to churches, palaces and paintings, and the use of a scarlet binding with gold-stamped titles were all hints from Murray.

In the space of a decade, the two houses, British and German (their genuine rivalry only began in 1860, when Baedeker started issuing his guides in English), effectively managed to standardize the guidebook as a literary form. As such, its validity was more readily acknowledged since it helped to replace, if never wholly to remove, the *cicerone*, that immemorial figure who had offered his services to the noblemen of the Grand Tour as they scrambled up and down the ruins of Rome, Pompeii and Paestum, and his avatars elsewhere on the Continent. Murray and Baedeker gave the modern tourist a decent sense of autonomy and freedom of choice, a chance to be selective over the precise amount of factual material he needed to absorb, and an opportunity to move at his own pace.

The tiresome prejudice in the English-speaking nations against the Germans for being German, something which, alas, will probably not have perished even with the last veteran of World War Two, means that it is all too easy for us to ridicule Baedeker's precision as quintessential Teutonic pedantry. We ought, instead of mocking such exhaustive thoroughness, to marvel at it, at the sheer prodigality and exuberance of the factual in which the anonymous compilers indulge, like grape-treaders at vintage dancing in vats overflowing with rich must. And on the subject of wine, the pages devoted to Bordeaux in Baedeker's *Southern France* offer as good an example as any of this abundance and generosity, of a continual readiness to provide us with more than we think we shall ever need to know.

My edition is dated 1914, and in this year there are five stations from which to enter the city, including one on a direct line through the Médoc vineyards. We can take a cab to the centre of town, and the flat bus fare is 50 centimes, with a 20-centime surcharge for a trunk. A motor taxi cost 1½ francs per thousand metres, but we may want to ride one of the fourteen electric trams whose routes are so thoughtfully provided in the book. Our room at the Hotel de France in Rue Esprit-des-Lois will cost 30 francs for full board. Only the French would name a street after a 500-page essay on the philosophy of law, but the guidebook will later remind us that its author Montesquieu graduated in jurisprudence here in 1708. We can draw money on letters of credit at the Comptoir d'Escompte in the Allées de Tourny, we can take a Turkish bath at the Thermes du Hammam in Rue Vital Carles, and if either of these activities should land us in any trouble, we can fall back on the assistance of A.L.S. Rowley, the British consul, or his American opposite number, A.K. Moe.

Baedeker displays a wonderful complicity with the travelling pontificator, the bore and know-it-all. Doubtless everyone is aware that the population of Bordeaux in 1914 is 261,678, that it is the head-quarters of the 18th army corps and the seat of an archbishopric, lying 60 miles from the Atlantic. But astonish your friends with the additional information that the city is the Gaulish Burdigala, capital of the Bituriges Vivisci, that in 1548 the imposition of the salt tax under Henri II caused a serious revolt, for which the town was punished by the Constable de Montmorenci, and that if you tip the guide 50 centimes in the crypt of St Michel he will show you forty natural mummies miraculously preserved by the action of the soil around the church.

Who dares doubt any of this? The anonymity of Baedeker guarantees its good faith. We trust these fat red volumes, with their 600-plus pages and minutely detailed folding maps, precisely because we don't know who compiled them or even who translated them into English. The Leipzig firm sold its books through T. Fisher Unwin in London and Scribner's in New York, but there is no authorial name to blame for possible errors. The author of the 1914 *Southern France* declares in all sincerity: 'Like the Editor's other handbooks, it is based on personal acquaintance with the country described, which has been specially revisited with a view to ensure accuracy and freshness of information. For the further improvement of this work, the Editor looks forward to a continuance of those valuable corrections and suggestions with which travellers have been in the habit of favouring him, and for which he is sincerely grateful. Their hotel bills, with annotations, are especially useful.'

Baedeker's namelessness gives it an Alpha-et-Omega authority. The emphatically personal utterance resounding through the pages of Murray's guides is equally persuasive. We believe these voices, hectoring, warning, spluttering, hissing, enthusing, romancing, expatiating or elaborating, to the extent that they become embodied for us, animated versions of those figures in some landscape of Edward Lear designed to give scale and verisimilitude to the prospect. In another book in my collection, *O'Shea's Spain*, produced in 1905 by the Edinburgh firm of A. & C. Black, the writer – Mr O'Shea presumably, though he fails to add a signature and his Christian name is never given – goes out of his way to signpost what he calls 'Prout bits' for each Spanish town. These morsels are named after the watercolourist Samuel Prout, admired for his characteristic sketches of picturesque nooks and corners in continental towns where the hand of the urban improver had not been too energetically applied. In Murray's handbooks the author always seems to me to be someone hanging about just out of the artist's range in a Prout bit. Those Spanish muleteers in their striped blankets, those Neapolitan beggar boys and Breton fishwives may fancy themselves safe, as decorative, costumed extras in the composition, but when Prout has moved off with his easel to find another bit, up will come Murray's man-with-a-notebook to chivvy them over loading the mules, curse them as arrant thieves, or demand directions to the harbour in best John Bull French.

It is Murray who, on landing in the Papal States in 1843, roundly curses the rapacity of the customs officers. First the traveller has to bargain with the porters – 'two pauls for landing are sufficient' (a paul was the basic unit of currency in the Pope's dominions) – then there are the luggage inspections, one by the gendarmes, the other by customs, each of whom must be paid a further two pauls. The British consul demands five pauls for a visa on every compatriot's passport, some of the fee ending up in the coffers of the police. On leaving the town, the wretched tourist has to fork out a further three pauls at the city gate. 'It will hardly be a matter of surprise,' says Murray, 'that in many instances the recollections of Civita Vecchia are not of the most agreeable kind.' When at length we reach Rome, where a further scattering of ten pauls is necessary if we are to avoid the customs house at Porta Cavalleggieri, our guide is voluble with warnings and recommendations. Try the fried lamb's brains at Scalinata in Piazza di Spagna – 'nearly all the most eminent English artists dine and sup here daily'. Make sure you enter your name in the address book at Galignani's English library. When asking for service at a café, strangers must call 'Bottega!' [shop] and not for the waiter if they wish to be served. Take lodgings in a street running from east to west, rather than north to south, as the latter is less exposed to currents of cold air. Remember, if giving a dinner for the nobility, that the Caetani take precedence over the Buoncompagni, that the Aldobrandini go before the Rospigliosi, that a foreign ambassador leads the way in front of a cardinal, and that a British nobleman only gives place to a prince.

The whole issue of the Roman aristocracy, at a period when the city itself was the capital of an independent sovereign state ruled by His Holiness the Pope, is one to which Murray devotes extensive column inches. There are important caveats as to the tendency of Italian city states to create their own nobilities without any reference to a more august authority. 'In thus dubbing plebeians with nobility, such municipalities have had no right to affix the titles which have, in so many instances, been abusively assumed, especially by foreigners, and by none more frequently than by our own countrymen, in general so avid of this kind of flimsy distinction.' There is a useful breakdown of the Papal peerage – 'about 180 persons under the general designation of the *Patriziato Romano*' – into princes and dukes (some of whom, Murray is quick to point out, 'have acquired their honours by the weight of their purses'), marquises and counts.

On these latter degrees the guide is severe. 'It is probable that several who bear these titles would find it difficult to exhibit their diplomas of creation: many derive them possibly from small feudal tenures.' Murray makes an exception here for the four families known as *Nobili del Baldacchino*, who possess, among other privileges, 'that of placing the feudal throne, with the blue parasol and kneeling cushion of the Princes and Dukes, in their ante-chambers'. The writer, identified only by the initials J.B.P., is particularly stern with the Italians as to their habit of using titles indiscriminately for every member of a noble clan. 'It is thus that as many as half-a-dozen Marquises and Counts may be found to belong to one family. The assumption of the title of Prince or Duke by the younger members of the baronial families, is equally unauthorized, although they will always rank by courtesy as Duke's sons, as in the British peerage.'

Murray's writer, you see, is a Somebody. He has ideas and takes a stand on everything. The hand-books, larger and more imposing than the squat, tubby little Baedekers, are emphatically personal in their approach. While the German guides take possession of various countries and regions through the sheer comprehensiveness involved in their trawl for knowledge, Murray's authors commandeer a given territory by dint of 'been there done that' experience. They may not know everything about a cathedral, a palace or a castle, but they are *knowing* about it in a fashion which manages to be both opinionated and insouciant at one and the same time.

The 'auteur' factor became an essential aspect of Murray's handbooks as the nineteenth century wore on. Many of Murray's writers, unlike J.B.P., chose to publish under their full names rather than seek the semi-anonymity of initials. Richard Ford was the first and in many ways the most distinguished of these when publishing his *Handbook to Spain* in 1845. In two volumes (though actually a reduction, in this form, of a much bulkier, more ambitious work), it constitutes one of the outstanding examples of the whole genre, a formidable achievement both in terms of its range – Ford rode over 2,000 miles on the same horse – and in the gusto with which the writer distils the alien exoticism of the country and its people for Murray's readers.

They were similarly privileged by *Central & Northern Japan* (1883), the work of Ernest Mason Satow and Lieutenant A.G.S. Hawes of the Royal Marines. Satow, consul-general in Bangkok and furnished with his CMG, had been legation secretary in Tokyo, having learned Japanese as a student interpreter and improved his knowledge of the language with the help of what was called in certain military and consular circles at the time 'a sleeping dictionary', in the form of a native mistress or *musume*, Takeda Kane, by whom he had two sons. In 1895, he became British minister plenipotentiary in Japan; his Murray volume, encyclopaedic in its range, is alas nowhere mentioned in the article devoted to him by the new *Oxford Dictionary of National Biography*.

The same work does better justice to Sir Lambert Playfair, author of the handbook for Algeria and Tunisia, issued in 1878. His grandfather was a Scottish geographer and his elder brother a pioneering chemist, whose researches into the Irish potato blight *Phytophthora infestans* were influential in encouraging Peel to repeal the corn laws, and whose experiments in extracting paraffin from naphtha found on a Derbyshire hillside laid the foundations of the modern petroleum industry. Lambert Playfair had similarly enquiring instincts. His *Algeria & Tunisia* is based on his experience as consul in various North African ports, on his knowledge of Berber dialects, on his journeys of exploration through the hinterland above the Sahara, and on the same kind of meticulousness which equipped him so well as the Maghreb's earliest major bibliographer.

Few of Murray's authors stamped their presence more emphatically on the reader than John Mason Neale. He is remembered as the author of favourite Anglican hymns such as 'Jerusalem the Golden', 'All glory, laud and honour' and 'Christ is made the sure foundation', not to speak of the favourite Christmas carol 'Good King Wenceslas'. Ordained in 1841, Neale became a leading figure in the Anglo-Catholic movement within the Church of England, the founding father of that great ecclesiological impulse which, whatever its mistakes and needless interferences, restored the beauty of holiness to many churches, saved others from wholesale destruction, and inspired some of the finest Victorian architectural projects. Once again the *DNB* article doesn't mention his Murray, the *Portugal* first published in 1854; more's the pity, since this is among the best in the whole series.

Portugal has seldom fared as well as it deserves at the hands of guidebook writers. Baedeker never condescends to award the country a volume to itself, preferring, like most other Iberian guides, to lump it together with Spain – an insult to any self-respecting Lusitanian or Lusophile. The 'practical hints' section for Portugal has a slightly glacial, if-we-really-must air about it which Baedeker is hardly at pains to suppress when we embark on the various tourist routes suggested for the country itself. On the railways, for example, though trains may run more punctually than in Spain, 'the stations are all primitive, the name boards are by no means conspicuous, and the vocal announcements of the names frequently indistinct'. Arriving in the various towns, travellers are warned against 'the touts of inferior hotels, the splendour of whose gold-laced caps is a very fallacious index to the comforts of the hostelries they represent'. Addressing such people in their native idiom is not recommended – 'the

Portuguese language makes a somewhat unpleasant impression on the visitor from Spain on account of the comparative dullness of its tone and the numerous sibilant and nasal sounds' – though Baedeker does its best with a guide to the mysteries of pronunciation in an extended footnote.

Murray's *Handbook for Travellers in Portugal* (1855), the first, and for a long time the only, freestanding English-language guide to the country, is a different affair altogether from Baedeker's later hole-in-corner treatment. It is alert from the outset to the fundamental truth (of which travellers still need reminding) that Portugal is not simply Spain in duodecimo, but a distinctive cultural experience within the same Iberian landmass. When J. M. Neale made his journey in 1853, amid a party of friends including the Scottish Episcopalian Bishop Forbes of Brechin and two other Tractarian clergymen, a distinctly epic atmosphere surrounded their travels. They were exploring a terrain more or less unknown to even the most adventurous Briton, with very little of that infrastructure of hotels, railways and French cookery on which the nineteenth-century tourist felt able to depend in more well-trodden areas of continental Europe. Portugal, what is more, had recently emerged from a civil war lasting almost twenty years. Furnishing home comforts for the sophisticated tourist – Anglican clergymen of the ritualist tendency were noted for their dainty habits and gourmet palates – must have been fairly low on the list of priorities in most Portuguese towns and villages.

The whole tone of Neale's *Portugal* combines the not-for-the-fainthearted aspects of today's Rough Guide and Lonely Planet series with the implication that it is always worth toughing out the disgusting food, the villainous wine, the verminous bedstraw in the mattresses, and the general air of desolation and emptiness among the upland towns of the Alentejo or Beira Alta purely for the sake of what lies over the hill or around the next bend. At Braga the inns may teem with fleas – Neale, with that typical Victorian fastidiousness which shrank from naming anything so physically intimate as a bloodsucking parasite, simply refers to them by the collective euphemism 'annoyance'. At Cape St Vincent the villages may be dirty and miserable, the fields covered in sand, the air in summer freezing, the roads 'scarcely practicable even for a mule'. Yet at the former place how lambent in its beauty the golden chalice in the sacristy – a Tractarian hymnodist was not proof against the sin of covetousness – how noble the organ in the choir, and what intense interest attached to the tomb of Saint Ovidius, third bishop of the diocese, to whom, before his conversion to Christianity, the poet Martial had sent a birthday epigram! As for Cape St Vincent, supposing your mule could actually get you there in one piece, 'the view will make amends for the wretchedness of the journey,' says Neale. 'This south-west angle of Europe is almost always stormy, but in a high gale the noise of the wind, whistling and shrieking in the convent, and the roar of the waves below, make it impossible to keep up a conversation.'

The guidebook's eternally despised status has meant that it has no specific literary classification, with the appropriate Greek-or-Latin-derived techno-logical jam label attached. The conceptual process involved in writing a travel guide bears no name like History, Biography, Fiction or Poetry under which we can categorize it as an art form. Yet in Murray's *Portugal* a powerful imagination is plainly at work. Neale has a clear idea of the particular kind of trav-eller he wants to engage with, and in this most per-sonal and idiosyncratic of guides the reader is, not surprisingly, an alter ego of the author. 'O hypocrite lecteur! Mon semblable, mon frère!' The figure in question is an enthusiast for church architecture and romantic landscapes; has no apprehensions as to riding for long distances over appalling roads on bad mounts with uncomfortable saddles; admires the honesty and courtesy of the native inhabitants; and does not assume that anyone he meets will speak a word of English.

A little way out of the city of Tomar, with its wonderful Renaissance convent of the Order of Christ, we reach the town of Punhete, at which point

Neale's voice suddenly sinks to an anxious whisper. 'The traveller must be careful not to inquire for the place by this name, as the slightest mispronunciation will convert it into one of the most vulgar words in the Portuguese language.' The word's official meaning is 'mitten' or 'small glove'; the slang interpretation may be easily imagined. We can grasp the nature of the writer's concern for that same language in one of the book's opening sections. From its forty-four pages of vocabulary and useful phrases, worlds both inner and outer spring to life. Anxiety initially predominates, in a flurry of questions. 'Are the beds made?'; 'How many baskets for half a crown?'; 'Is Mr O. at home?'; 'Is he lame?'; 'Should I leave a card?'; 'Where is my whip?'; 'What is the price of ducks?'; 'Why don't you answer me?'

Neale's imagined tourist, in the columns of his Portuguese vocabulary, is sharp with the servants. 'Never come into my room without knocking.' 'Go early to market.' 'I want a rice pudding.' 'I don't like the smell of tobacco in the house.' As a Puseyite clergyman should be, he is familiar with the habits of good society – 'Will you do me the honour to dance the next waltz with me?' – but experience has clearly taught him not to expect too much of the Portuguese households he is likely to end up in. 'The razors are blunt.' 'The pillows are hard.' 'These sheets are damp.' ' I could not sleep because the dog barked so.'

As Rose Macaulay (herself fond of Tractarians) noted in a chapter devoted to Neale in her classic *They Went to Portugal*, a major part of the phrase list is devoted to horses, since the traveller will have to ride most of the way. There is everything here from the Portuguese for bay, chestnut and piebald to snaffle, crupper and martingale. Neale's imagined horse has as much character as his rider: 'Don't leave him alone !' 'There, he's off!' 'He is lazy.' 'He is short-winded.' 'He is not master of my weight.' 'Is he playful?' 'He has an easy mouth.' 'He is a jibber.' 'The horse is of unequalled strength, has sparkling eyes, and possesses no vice.'

—

The archetypal Victorian guidebook auteur was that singular figure, almost resistant to categorization of any sort – the word 'writer' does him no justice whatever – Augustus J.C. Hare. Born in 1834 in Rome (appropriately, as it turned out), he was almost at once deemed superfluous to family requirements. 'Both my father and Mrs Hare were greatly annoyed at the birth of another child,' he later wrote, 'and beyond measure disgusted that it was another son.' This role of extra, adjunct or makeweight was to be Hare's destiny, in one form or another, for the rest of his life, though many others would take more delight in his company than at first his parents did. Soon after his christening, which took place in the Hares' rented villa on the slopes of the Viminal, Augustus was begged for by his childless aunt Maria, widow of the paternal uncle after whom he was named. 'My dear Maria, how very kind of you!' ran his mother's answering letter. 'Yes, certainly, the baby shall be sent to you as soon as it is weaned; and if any one else would like one, would you kindly recollect that we have others?'

Aunt Maria had retreated to Sussex, to live in the shadow of another of her brothers-in-law, the severely evangelical Reverend Julius Hare, who enlivened his labours as Archdeacon of Lewes with periodic attempts at disciplining the borrowed son with a riding whip. Oddly, despite a childhood involving often grotesque extremes of misery and privation in the name of character-building, Augustus came to love his aunt so much that he considered her a more genuine mother than the bored expatriate in Rome, who had so cheerfully dumped him at the earliest opportunity. Delicious puddings snatched away when still hot on the table, rhubarb-and-soda administered as a punishment for eating a lollipop, further chastisement given for daring to ask local children to tea, entire days spent in silence, and occasional imprisonment in the freezing vestry of the parish church with only rats and skulls for company – all such details form part of one of those survival narratives in which the annals of nineteenth-century English childhood are so horrifyingly rich.

The ignorance, priggishness, and cruelty of Aunt Maria, Uncle Julius, and the loathsome governess Esther Maurice – a creature diabolical beyond anything imagined by Dickens or the Brontës – were offset for little Augustus by occasional visits to kinder, more indulgent relatives in Shropshire and the Lake District. Very quickly the boy seems to have developed a talent, on such trips, for nosing out and cultivating celebrities, which remained with him in adulthood, throughout a life of being never in the way and never out of it on country house weekends, making up the number at a London dinner party from which some more glamorous guest had cried off, or shadowing various European royal highnesses as a discreet tutorial companion on their travels through Italy and France. He was friendly with Victorian movers and shakers such as Matthew Arnold, Benjamin Jowett, Dean Stanley and Angela Burdett Coutts, and he dined with the Empress Frederick and Prince Leopold, and hobnobbed with the likes of Gladstone and Lord Salisbury. Recalling these and other leading figures of the age, Hare eventually sat down to write his memoirs, further enlivened with much piquant drawing-room gossip and items from his well-stocked collection of true ghost stories, cramming everything into the three enormous volumes published as *The Story of My Life* in 1896. He died seven years later, at what was even then the relatively early age of sixty-nine. When an abridged two-part edition appeared in 1953, its text skilfully interwoven with passages from his journals, its intrinsic value as a guide to the eminent Victorianness of the Victorian era was at once established. The two volumes, entitled *The Years with Mother* and *In My Solitary Life*, so abundantly entertaining as they are, should never have been allowed to go out of print.

Augustus Hare had undoubted limitations. He was a snob, valuing his family's grander connections and delighting in the condescension of royalty and the nobility. His engaging indiscretion was matched by a personal fearfulness which was essentially that of the deeply suppressed homosexual, for whom even the most extended visit to the Continent could never be enlivened, as far as we know, by vigorous intercourse with gondoliers, fisherboys, guardsmen or waiters. In many ways, he can be viewed simply as a useful extra in a Victorian panorama already crowded to bursting with talent, vitality and inventiveness, a figure eternally on the edge, somebody in the back row of one of those group photographs taken on the terraces and lawns of country houses during the 1870s and 1880s, with men wearing rakishly cocked bowlers and women got up like expensively upholstered armchairs.

There is one gift, however, for which Hare deserves to be remembered, apart from his skills as an anecdotalist and social chronicler. In 1859 he began work on a guidebook, one of Murray's English series, to the three adjacent counties of Berkshire, Buckinghamshire and Oxfordshire. The success of this secured him a further commission from the same publisher, for a volume on County Durham. Others would surely have followed if his surrogate mother Aunt Maria had not been in need of a warmer climate for her failing health. The pair set off for an indefinite sojourn in France and Italy.

Contact had never been lost with Hare's biological mother, Anne Frances, whom as a child he had nicknamed 'Italima' – 'Italian mamma' – and who still lived in the Rome whence she had bundled him off, thirty-odd years previously, as an infant inconvenience. During a visit there, soon after he left Oxford, he had renewed the acquaintance, clinching what was, in essence, a close friendship rather than an orthodox familial bond. Perhaps inevitably, she had converted at last to Roman Catholicism, enjoying, like many others 'going over' in the age of Wiseman, Newman and Manning, the forms and ceremonies of her new church, their various picturesque and historic resonances, and the social cachet acquired through her apostasy. In Rome itself she whisked Augustus off to balls at Palazzo Borghese and dinners with Queen Cristina, former regent of Spain and great-niece of Marie Antoinette. At the Borghese parties the Hares paid court to the dowager principessa, née La Rochefoucauld, a fearsome old harpy rumoured to have poisoned her son's first wife and their children in order to clear the way for his marriage to her niece. While the guests danced in the frescoed saloon, a scatter of cardinals sat down to a game of whist in an adjacent room.

One day Italima took her son to a private audience with Pope Pius IX, 'a sturdy figure with a beneficent face, in what looked like a white dressing gown'. The pair were accompanied by Hare's sister Anne, known as Esmeralda, a girl he had hardly known until now. Getting acquainted with her was, he says, 'to me like the perpetual reading of an engrossing romance, for nobody was ever more amusing, no one ever had more power of throwing an interest into the commonest things of life. She did not colour her descriptions but she saw life through a prism, and imparted its rays to others.' On this occasion it was Esmeralda who broke the ice with Pope Pius, after the requisite sequence of genuflections (Augustus counted nine) and ring-kissings, by announcing that her brother insisted on remaining a Protestant. His Holiness gave this obstinate heretic a little lecture on the blessings of Roman Catholicism, making it clear that, as far as he was concerned, Hare was unworthy of sharing them. Then he asked him earnestly to promise that he would always remember to say the Lord's Prayer each morning. Apparently unaware that this was a regular practice among a good many Anglicans at that period, he enjoined Augustus to reflect on the words 'Thy will be done on earth as it is in heaven', adding 'Remember that you have promised this at the feet of Pope Pius IX.'

As things turned out there was to be no going-over for Augustus. Aunt Maria's Protestant influence proved to have tougher roots than Italima's Popery. Hare's already considerable suspicion of the new wave of English Romanists and their motives was strengthened after Esmeralda died in London from a lingering illness, when he became involved in a most disagreeable lawsuit with a ring of her avaricious co-religionists over the terms of a will in their favour she had annulled on her deathbed, but whose clauses they sought to establish as still binding. His visits to Rome itself were nevertheless enjoyable and he would always prefer the atmosphere of the city as papal capital, a venerable little walled town of ruins, churches, and palaces among verdant gardens, to its brash new incarnation, after 1870, as metropolis of the Kingdom of Italy, all clanging trams and dusty boulevards.

Successive trips were varied by exploring what were then such wilder reaches of Italy as the Marche, the Abruzzi and the Maremma region of south-west Tuscany. Out of these Italian wanderings Hare evolved an entirely new species of guidebook, one which combined the discreet presence of the author as *cicerone* and ambulant art historian with copious extracts (printed in a smaller font size than the surrounding text) drawn from modern writers, such as Théophile Gautier, Horatio Brown, Anna Jameson and the invaluable Ruskin, or from the Italian chroniclers and poets of an earlier age. Volumes in the series – and though not conceived as such it soon became one – can still be used with pleasure in such sacred spots as Florence's San Miniato al Monte or the Doge's Palace in Venice. Rambling through the latter's halls and corridors, Hare offers not just the pertinent aperçus from *Modern Painters* and *The Stones of Venice* but little snatches of Dickens, Casanova and George Eliot as well. At San Miniato, the writer's enthusiasm provides a vitamin shot for the traveller bursting in upon this most arrestingly lambent of church interiors. Lapped by its 'cool twilight', we savour the 'exquisite *transenna* panelled out in fourteen sections of marble mosaic and relief-designs', the frieze around the Medici chapel, 'prettily inlaid in black and white', 'the deep choir' and the 'primitive and limited' illumination from the round-headed lights within the clerestory.

Then of course there's the view, even today one of the finest cityscapes in the whole world. 'And now,' says Hare, plucking us delicately by the sleeve, 'let us enjoy the enchanting prospect from the door. For yonder, immediately below us to the right, lies Florence in all her beauty, with her Duomo set calmly upon her like a dim red crown, while beyond and behind, flank after sloping flank of purple and fainter purple, mountains descend to the scented plain, as it were, like the Magi of old, on bending knees: and to the left, again, ridge after green ridge of villa-crowned hills succeeds in carrying the eye onward and upward to the lofty Apennines and the sunset.' Was it all ever more ardently evoked?

Nowadays we can mock the bejewelled sub-Ruskinian prose, with its obvious indebtedness – even if the setting here is Tuscan – to those enraptured descriptions, by that earlier writer, of Torcello or of the approach to Venice from Fusina by gondola. This, in its vulgarest form, was the sort of thing derided by E.M. Forster in *A Room with a View*, the pinchbeck portentousness which gave the likes of Charlotte Bartlett, Eleanor Lavish and the Reverend Cuthbert Eager a necessary rhetoric for overcoming the aesthetic challenges posed by the work of Fra Angelico, Donatello and Ghiberti. Hare's 'scented plain' may nowadays be full of exhaust fumes from lorries thundering along the *tangenziali* and *superstrade*, freighted with bidets and bathroom tiles from the factories of Calenzano and Scandicci, but his ecstasy is, fortunately, still something we can share.

His guidebooks do not limit themselves to the purely rhapsodic. Their candour in voicing disapproval, contempt or disgust is always noteworthy. The 'General Information' pages at the opening of his *Venice* convey an instant idea of the sort of traveller – sophisticated, inquisitive and exacting – at whom the volume and its companions are aimed. Among listed hotels such as the Danieli, the Europa and the Monaco, a warning note is sounded with the Vittoria – 'on a side canal, good, but overrun by "Cook's Tourists"'. In the days before widespread environmental awareness, Hare has a good word to offer for the *vaporetto*, the water bus so deeply loathed by Ruskin – 'much abused, but really no disfigurement, and a great convenience'. Which is more than can be said for the various Venetians jostling each other to show foreigners around the city. 'Guides are unusually ignorant, vulgar and stupid at Venice, and all but the most hopelessly imbecile travellers will find them an intolerable nuisance.'

When the first of Hare's books was published, John Murray, to whose own series their author was a former contributor, scented uncomfortable new competition. Matters came to a head in 1875, when what Hare, not without smugness, calls 'my three thick volumes of the *Cities of Northern and Central Italy*' received a first printing of 3,000 copies. Murray went on to the attack with a magazine review berating Hare for plagiarism and was soon joined by Edward Augustus Freeman, the distinguished historian of the Norman Conquest. Irritated at discovering that the book lifted material from a series of articles he had recently written on Italian cities, Freeman now gathered these together in a single volume, with a preface accusing Hare of theft. The beleaguered guidebook-writer was forced to issue a face-saving statement in no fewer than sixteen newspapers, but subsequently consoled himself, in the pages of *The Story of My Life*, by declaring that Freeman's articles had initially been ignored 'owing to the unpopularity of the dogmatic and verbose style in which they written', and that the cannibalizing of them for *Cities of Northern and Central Italy* was merely doing the Oxford history professor a good turn.

The popularity of Hare's guides was well justified. They were properly researched, generously informative and – as Freeman and Murray had cause to complain – more than adequately furnished with background material for works of art, buildings and historical events. They were also, in the case of the smaller volumes such as *Florence, Venice* and *Walks in Rome*, designed for practical use by travellers at large in the city. Much of their art-historical wisdom has obviously been rendered obsolete during the past hundred years: a pronouncement like that on the painter Jacopo Bassano, for example – 'His works have very little of variety or invention. He chiefly excelled in portraits' – is, thank goodness, no longer acceptable. Yet Augustus Hare deserves adequate recognition as the founder, for Anglophone readers, of that particularly congenial handbook genre best represented in our own day by the much-admired

Companion Guide series published by Collins (now HarperCollins) during the 1960s and 1970s. In works such as these, we walk the hallowed ground a little like the young Tobias in the Apocryphal Book of Tobit, with the writer acting as our guardian angel Raphael, always nudging us towards the next good thing.

—

Unlike J. M. Neal in Murray's *Portugal*, Augustus Hare does not see any need to include a section devoted to useful phrases in the language of the country visited, probably assuming that the sort of British or American traveller likely to make use of these works would have picked up some Italian or French anyway. The market for independently produced phrasebooks grew exponentially with that of the guidebook. Most of them followed the pattern, unchanged since Elizabethan times, of providing specialist vocabularies on dress, food, journeys and accommodation, followed by specimen conversations arranged like miniature dramas, envisaging the various situations in which travellers might find themselves during the trip. One or two of these manuals offer help with pronunciation. In *The French Pronouncing Handbook*, published in 1853, A.G.C. Jobert, author of *Le Trésor de Pensées* and *La Philosophie de la Géologie*, plays the role of a Gallic Professor Higgins. Here the various conversations are rendered phonetically for the English speaker. 'Donnay-mwooah une trawnch de daingdong si voo play'; 'Une kweesse de faysong'; 'Pahsai-mwooah ung per de so-see-song'; and so on. Doubtless the Englishman at Mr Podsnap's dinner party in Dickens's *Our Mutual Friend*, whose attempt at conversation with a French guest was limited to a word he pronounced as 'Esker', could have done with help from Jobert.

The *French Pronouncing Handbook* also offered useful advice, at the end of the volume, on how to get the best out of a visit to Paris (Pahree). Those with money to burn could take apartmang-zah-looai in the Shangz-aileezai or Lah Shosay dangtaing, tourists of moderate income were recommended to settle in Foboor Saing Jairmaing, and bachelors of small means might bed down comfortably near the Luksangboor or the Jahrdaing dai Plangt. Jobert's is one of the earliest of guides to cater explicitly for the budget tourist end of the market. Those without sufficient funds, but eager to sample the fare at smart restaurants like the Café de Paris on the Boulevard des Italiens or Vefour in the Palais-Royal, are urged, if there is more than one of them at dinner, to order only a single dish between them for each course – 'poor ung', don't you know. Jobert explains: 'So you have a comfortable dinner for half the expense marked on the carte. If you dine alone at prix fixe (pree fix) establishments, you will almost invariably be served, for two francs or two and a half francs, hard and unpalatable meat; whilst in following the plan we have pointed out, you will have first-rate French cuisine (kweezeen) for the same price.' A certain Miss James of 91, Clande Road, Cardiff, who owned *The French Pronouncing Handbook* a considerably long time before I acquired her copy at a second-hand bookshop in Cheltenham, marked this whole section with a pair of emphatic – and, one assumes, approving – crosses.

Murray and Baedeker were quick to provide their own phrasebooks. The former's *Handbook of Travel Talk*, published in 1874, takes a characteristically downright approach to the whole business of getting the traveller going in the three different languages provided, German, French and Italian. The author 'does not pretend, as some do, to enable Englishmen abroad to talk a foreign language without having opened a grammar beforehand. That would be an absurdity. Hitherto such essential topics as "Custom House", "Railway Station", "Telegraphs", "Passports", and "Tea-Making" have scarcely been alluded to in books of this class. The Dialogues will be found, of necessity, to contain more questions than answers, as it is not possible to anticipate what may be the different modes of reply to an inquiry.'

The specialist vocabularies satisfy far more than basic needs. We learn the German for a flying buttress, 'Streteboken'; the French for machicolation, 'machicoulis'; and the Italian for rood screen, 'tribuna'. The section headed 'Some Terms of French Cookery Explained' includes 'Compiègne – a sweet yeast cake with fruit', 'Godiveau – a savoury pie' and 'Financière – an expensive highly-flavoured mixed ragout'. In the dialogues, we sit down to a game of chess ('Your queen is well supported'; ' I am afraid this castle is lost'), we climb mountains ('It has frozen: we must cut steps in the ice'); we buy a carriage ('the cushions are not well stuffed'); we argue with our washerwoman ('Are you the laundress of the house? There is a handkerchief missing'); and we quiz our dressmaker ('Do they still wear flounces?' 'Oh yes, Madam. Would you like the body trimmed with lace?' 'No, I don't like it, it spoils the figure').

An entire world stands disclosed within these books, most of them now extremely rare, as phrase-books get junked even more readily than guide-books. Murray's obvious model – a rip-off, in fact – was Baedeker's *Traveller's Manual of Conversation*, which went into several editions without much altering its basic material. In its columns the tele-graph office remained 'the electric telegraph office' for many years, cobblers still supplied top-boots, and tailors continued making nankeen pantaloons long after the fashion for these articles had died out. Conversation in Baedeker is more voluble and sharply characterized than in Murray. At supper, for example: 'John, snuff the candles and give me the oil. What is that you are bringing?' 'A pike which was swimming in the river five hours ago.' 'I shall be very well placed opposite the Countess. Will you allow me to help you to some vermicelli?' 'No, thank you. I ate it so good in Italy, that I do not choose to run the risk of eating it bad in France.'

Baedeker's English here, hardly idiomatic, is a more or less literal rendering of the original German. It is amid these richly enjoyable pages – the whole work, by the way, could do with a modern reprint – that I suspect I may have tracked down the origin of an urban myth. In the sections devoted to travel there are several references to postilions. 'Are the postilions insolent? No, never when they are paid', etcetera. In their company, the journey is not without incident. 'Is the road safe? Do you ever hear of robbers?' Just before these dialogues comes one on the weather. 'It rains in torrents, it thunders, it lightens, it hails.' Have I stumbled across the earliest glimmer of that legendary phrasebook item which in one version is supposed to run 'The postilion has been struck by lightning', and in another, yet more implausible, 'Ho, postilion, I have been struck by lightning'?

—

While the content and layout of these phrasebooks tell us much about the psycho-sociological baggage

of the Victorian traveller, the guidebooks themselves are full of solicitous advice as to the physical
impedimenta wanted on the voyage. Satow and
Hawes, amid their hundred-plus pages of introductory material on Japan, go into considerable detail on
the basic needs of travellers in the Mikado's realm.
They begin, most sensibly, by urging us to get rid of
trunks and boxes in favour of 'the Japanese wicker
baskets called *yanagi-gori*, in every way the most
capacious and portable'. Together with Western
dress, we should pack Japanese loose cotton *yukata*
gowns and a *san jaku* sash to tie them with. An air
pillow, a sun hat and a plaid, shawl or rug for sleeping in the mountains will come in handy, as will
extra boot laces ('hippopotamus hide are best'), an
aneroid barometer, carbolic acid, and 'Persian insect
powder'. The usefulness of going native is further
emphasized with a recommendation to order at least
a dozen pairs of *waraji*, straw sandals, for wading
streams. 'With them are worn Japanese socks, *tabi*,
which should be made of the dark blue cloth known
as *mekura-jima*. A supply of two or three sets of
strings should be taken; the best are made of hemp
dyed with indigo.' For those accustomed to Japanese
food but wary of country inns, meals could be made
from a tin or two of Liebig's Beef Extract, something
called German Pea-Soup Sausage, Chicago Corned
Beef, and a bottle of Worcestershire Sauce.

Liebig's and Lea & Perrins are essential brand names in many a similar list of fall-back supplies for gastronomic emergencies. Other kinds of relief were offered by Fry's Cocoa, Dinneford's Fluid Magnesia, Keating's Powder and Rowland's Odonto Toothpaste. For those mistrustful of foreign food on the well-established basis of its foreignness, there was comfort to hand in a variety of tins and packets. Crosse & Blackwell's soups and potted meats could be stowed among the wraps, mufflers, footwarmers, bootjacks, buttonhooks, spare stay-laces, spencers and Norfolk jackets somewhere in the capacious trunk, along with McDoddie's dried vegetables. 'The McDoddie Pure British Vegetables (Dry)' seems to conjure up some picture of a crabbit laird in a kilt and tam o'shanter. 'Not only are the true flavours of the vegetables preserved, but what is just as important, the peculiar chemical conditions of the food constituents are unchanged by the process. One pound of McDoddie vegetables is equivalent to about 12lbs of fresh. Require no soaking, and when cooked cannot be distinguished from the fresh – Cabbage, Carrots, Celery, French Beans, Julienne, Parsnips, Stick Rhubarb, Turnips etcetera in ½lb, 1lb and 2lb lever-top canisters.'

Baedeker and Murray are scrupulously pre-scriptive as to clothing and equipment, wherever the tourist should happen to find himself. For those going to Sweden in 1875 a portable India-rubber bath was required, and visitors to Lapland in August should take a mosquito veil 'long enough, after being tied round the hat, for the other end to tuck into the waistcoat'. Murray's *Knapsack Guide to Norway* adds to these a knife, fork and spoon, candles, the inevitable Liebig's, mustard and tea. If the tourist is to bring a dog along (no quarantine laws were then in force) the animal 'may be carried in a net or a bag slung under the carriage, upon the Italian plan. It is always the safest way to carry a dog in that manner, in case of his being attacked by a wolf, for with that animal a dog is an irresistible temptation.'

As we move further east, the sense of fuss and near-desperation by the writer on our behalf increases. In Greece, Baedeker recommends flannel shirts, puttees for riding breeches, a puggaree round the crown of the hat, 'smoke-coloured spectacles' and a stout cane to drive off savage dogs. A local guide or dragoman is indispensable, and the author reprints the entire text, in French, of a written contract for such services. 'Less exacting travellers, especially those who are young and vigorous,' says Baedeker, 'may dispense with this expensive luxury and content themselves with an *agoyatis*, an ordinary horse-boy. In concluding the agreement with him, known as *symphonia*, which is best done in a café over a cup of coffee, the traveller should preserve an air of indifference and avoid all indications of hurry.'

Once we cross the borders of Christendom into the Orient, foreigners become more tricky. Neither Ernest Satow in Murray's *Japan* nor Colonel H.C. Fanshawe in the *India, Burma & Ceylon* handbook for 1907, seems to have any idea that his readers will want to do anything so outlandish as to meet the inhabitants of these respective countries on a social level. In guides to Egypt and Syria, on the other hand, Baedeker includes a section intriguingly headed 'Intercourse with Orientals'. 'The average Oriental regards the European as a Croesus, and sometimes too as a madman, so unintelligible to him are the objects and pleasures of travelling,' it begins. 'He should bear in mind,' the advice goes on, 'that many of the natives with whom he comes in contact are mere children, whose demands should excite amusement rather than anger. On the other hand, intimate acquaintance with Orientals is to be avoided, disinterested friendship being still rarer in the east than elsewhere.'

If stepping westwards to the USA, the traveller was faced with different challenges altogether from those posed by an over-assiduous dragoman or a mob of fellaheen demanding baksheesh. At the start of a 'General Hints' section in Baedeker's 1904 *United States* we can detect an invitation to read between the lines. 'The first requisites for the enjoyment of a tour in the United States are an absence of prejudice and a willingness to accommodate oneself to the customs of the country. If the traveller exercise a little patience, he will often find that ways which strike him as unreasonable or even disagreeable are more suitable to the environment than those of his own home would be.' Hereafter, we learn that American cities have dirty streets, overcrowded public transport, overpriced goods in their shops and a lack of public conveniences (especially in New York). Americans themselves drive on the right and spit on the floor.

Intercourse here presents almost as many pitfalls as in Egypt, but these are mostly linguistic. The guide helpfully supplies a glossary of a hundred-odd words 'in frequent use in the United States in a sense not commonly known in England'. Some of these, such as 'tuxedo', 'sophomore', 'highball' and 'elevator' (for 'lift') are still indicators of the demarcation line between British and American English. But it may surprise us to find that 'chore', 'shortage', 'lovely' and 'wilt' were all regarded as Americanisms in 1904. An American takes a lady 'out' to dinner while an Englishman takes her 'in'; the habit of referring to a male chicken as a cock offends transatlantic ears accustomed to 'rooster'; and on no account should the word 'nasty', meaning 'disgusting' in America, be used in polite company.

—

The image of the Victorian and Edwardian tourist

gradually emerging from the books I have been discussing possesses two different dimensions. One of these tends to flatter a somewhat patronizing, how-different-from-us, bless-their-hearts-weren't-they-quaint view of our ancestors. Such a perspective is conditioned by the idea of a chain of social Darwinism reaching its notional apogee in existing generations around the start of the twenty-first century, and I own, looking back over certain comments made here, that my essay is not wholly free of this.

The other aspect is altogether distinct from this one – embarrassingly so, we might almost say. In the *Muqadimmah*, his great introduction to the philosophy of history, composed in 1377, the Tunisian historian Ibn Khaldun reminds us that 'the past resembles the present as one drop of water another'. We confront the reproachfully obvious truth of this statement when placing the modern traveller alongside his or her nineteenth-century avatar and realizing, in the process, how few changes have taken place in the basic profile over the intervening hundred years. The limitations, fears and prejudices are identical. There is the same reaching after a comprehensiveness of experience, an ambition to absorb more than we can logically consume, the same challenges are issued to curiosity and ignorance, there are the same competitive attitudes towards sightseeing and a comparable desire on the traveller's part to get it all right, if possible to the point of protective mimicry, where the etiquette and customs of the natives are involved, so long as these people are Christian, wear trousers and skirts and eat with knives and forks.

What the guidebooks also furnish in abundance is evidence of the speed with which tourism assumed the outlines of the global industry it has now become. A fascinating question, in the present context, is that of how far the availability of printed guides and the contribution made by their authors to the idea of the tourist as consumer actually influenced this development, either in its extent or in the particular directions it chose to take. Murray's business acumen meant that almost from the outset each of the handbooks in the series could be self-financing with the help of advertising supplements bound in at either end of the volume. Their publicity for hotels everywhere from Aachen to Zurich is as deserving of careful scrutiny as the text itself, once we've ceased being dazzled by the copywriter's hyperbole or captivated by engravings showing forecourts perfectly thronged with smart carriages, in the act either of unloading or of whisking away the satisfied guests. So many first-class establishments, so many choice wines, reasonable prices, magnificent situations, omnibuses to meet the trains, hydraulic lifts, warm baths, perfect sanitary arrangements, à-la-carte breakfasts and lawn tennis courts, not to speak of invigorating mountain air, Bengal lights to illuminate the waterfalls, patronage from their Imperial Majesties the Emperor and Empress of Brazil, polite and ready attendance, winter gardens, shelter against the mistral, best stag and roebuck shooting, billiard room with Thurston's Tables and, for many the greatest comfort of all, 'English church service in the hotel'.

The presence of an Anglican church, or at least an Anglican minister to lead prayers in the designated saloon, is a continual selling point among Murray's advertisers, reminding us that British and (following the end of their Civil War) American tourists provided the mainstay of international hotel patronage during the nineteenth century's closing decades. Most self-respecting establishments boasted 'English spoken' among their attractions. In Athens, the Grand Hotel d'Angleterre employed 'Angelo Melissino, the well-known interpreter to English Visitors', St Petersburg's Hotel d'Angleterre provided 'Guides and Servants Speaking English', and in Moscow the Swiss proprietor of the Hotel Berlin was at pains to point out that he had formerly been engaged by the Midland Hotel attached to London's St Pancras Station.

Yet for all this eager solicitation of Anglophone custom, the guidebook writers were thoroughly conscious of the ways in which their compatriots made themselves obnoxious, or at least ridiculous, in different corners of the world, through their meanness, ignorance, tactlessness and highhandedness. Interestingly in this regard, the introductory material for the fourteenth edition of Murray's *Handbook for Travellers in France* (1877) includes a section headed 'The English Abroad' whose author lays about him, in no uncertain terms, at boorish John Bull let loose on continental Europe. Such unpopularity 'in the first place arises from the number of ill-conditioned persons ("mauvais sujets") who, not being in a condition to face the world at home, scatter themselves over foreign lands and bring no little discredit on their country'. The anonymous critic goes on to berate those who, 'through inattention, unguardedness, wanton expenditure in some cases, niggardly parsimony in others', bring their own nation into disrepute.

Some of Howell's advice to his seventeenth-century English voyagers is pertinently echoed, two hundred years later, by Murray. 'If an Englishman were fully aware how much it increases the pleasure and profit of travelling to have made some progress in foreign languages before he sets foot on the Continent, no one would think of quitting home until he had devoted at least some months to hard labour with grammars and dictionaries.' More trenchant still is the reproof administered to arrogant English Protestants who laugh and chatter during Catholic church services, turn their backs on the altar and stroll down the aisles arm-in-arm with ladies, 'a practice contrary to respect and good breeding'. We are reminded of the outraged embarrassment endured by the actress Frances Kemble, who, visiting St Peter's in Rome one Sunday during the 1820s, saw a party of fashionably attired Britons, concealed behind a pillar, unpacking a picnic hamper and popping champagne corks during the celebration of mass. She was hardly the first traveller, and would certainly not be the last, who wished, at such moments, that they belonged to any other nation than England.

Here and there throughout Murray's advertising supplements we find faint indications that some of the tourists being so extravagantly solicited may in fact have been female. The Hotel Beau Rivage at Lucerne and the Bellevue at Dresden offer 'Ladies' Parlours', while the Queen's Hotel, Penzance, has a 'Ladies' Coffee Room'. Neale's Portuguese phrasebook features a short but telling selection of terms relating to feminine attire – 'Bring me my cotton stockings', 'Lace my stays tighter', etcetera – and Baedeker's *Paris* for 1900 condescends so far as to assume the presence of women visitors in the world capital of fashion. Even so, the guide's advice is scarcely encouraging. 'Strangers should avoid shops in which "English spoken" is announced, as the English-speaking shopman is almost always "temporarily absent" and the use of English only invites an attempt to fleece the foreigners.' Any ideas an adventurous female tourist might have as to 'seeing life' in one of the more atmospheric Parisian locales are firmly knocked on the head. At the *cabarets artistiques*, 'the entertainments, which consist of songs, mystic illusions, shadow-plays etc., are often clever, but presuppose a considerable knowledge of colloquial French. These cabarets are scarcely suitable for ladies.' Neither were the dances held at the Moulin-Rouge and the Moulin de La Galette, while 'at many of the theatres, ladies are not admitted to the orchestra stalls, the space between each row of seats being so narrow that even gentlemen have some difficulty in passing in and out'.

—

By the beginning of the twentieth century, the concept of tourism projected by the guidebooks had moved far beyond the simple idea of travelling for the sake of notching up 'lions' – the word was applied to sights as well as celebrities – or capturing 'Prout bits' with the aid of cartridge paper and a box of Windsor & Newton's moist watercolours. One of the newer incarnations of the wanderer was as hunter and fisherman. Lambert Playfair, in his *Algeria & Tunisia*, includes a review of sporting opportunities in North Africa. Wild game, he notes, is fast disappearing in Algeria, since 'the country is becoming too settled'. He appends a table of French colonial government rewards offered for the destruction of various animals - lions and panthers at 40 francs, hyenas at 15 and jackals at 2. Hunting is still to be had of wild boar, gazelle, partridge and bustard, however, and if we make friends with the French army officers in the forts along the edge of the Sahara, they may offer to take us to an Arab falconry display.

Where good fishing was sought, the inland waters of Sweden and Norway were the playgrounds, by 1870, of those for whom British trout and salmon were becoming insufficiently abundant or worthy of trophy status. Murray was now recommending the fish in Sweden's Lake Wettern or the rivers of Dalecarlia, and pointing out that in Norway an English angler in 1847 had hooked 2,500 pounds weight of salmon in the river Alten in fourteen days. For hunters, the Scandinavian forests and fells were just waiting to be plundered. The elk-shooting season stretched from August to November, hares were safe only during the high summer months, and reindeer could roam securely between March and September. Bounties were offered by the government for wolves, lynxes, eagles and hawks, but the ultimate souvenir from a Norwegian tour was a bear skin. Murray, however, has no illusions as to the danger of close encounters with bears. Always take a dog and use a large-bore shotgun. When the animal charges, lie face down on the ground and breathe as little as possible. Bear flesh is not the best eating, but almost anything else we might bag can enliven a dull dinner in a country inn. 'Beef stewed to a jelly and poured into the windpipes of oxen becomes quite hard and never turns mouldy; an inch of this put into a small camp-kettle with the game or wild fowl, and vegetables of any kind, makes an admirable dish.'

More significant, however, than sportsmen as a tourist constituency were the invalids, hypochondriacs or those incorrigible epicures in need of drying out and irrigation after months of over-eating. The whole phenomenon of health holidays, developing from the pervasive culture of the English seaside resort and the German spa, had become a major industry. Over a wide range of illnesses, removal from one climate to another constituted the only available therapy. A medical regime could be followed less easily amid the metropolitan temptations of London, Paris or Berlin than in the context of a daily routine involving constant social contact with fellow sufferers, the continual presence of doctors and nurses, a restful *mise en scène* made up of hotels like thinly disguised hospitals, and a timetable of moderate exercise, spare diet, early bed, and no strenuous amusements.

The benefits of spas, watering places and winter destinations form a leitmotif in later editions of the

Victorian guidebooks. There is nothing, it seems, that a bubbling fountain – hot, cold, iron-tasting or sulphur-stinking – cannot heal. Royat-les-Bains, near Clermont-Ferrand, will help sufferers from throat infections, anaemia and gout; Vernet, in the Pyrenees, cures skin ailments, neuralgia and sciatica; and the sodium-chloride-impregnated waters of Bourbonne, in the Marne valley, are efficacious in treating scrofula, rheumatism, old gunshot wounds, and paralysis. Bad Ems, on the German river Lahn, is known euphemistically as a 'ladies' bath', and for gallstones and diabetes we visit Bad Neuenahr. Our over-generous waistlines will be packed in volcanic mud at Elster, south of Leipzig, with its 218 bathrooms; for our nerves we repair to Oeynhausen's salt springs; but perhaps the sheer size of the hotels in Wiesbaden, rather than the waters themselves, will be what helps us to recover from the dyspepsia whose cure is said to be on tap there.

The cult of the water cure is one of the most significant features of nineteenth-century life. Though the practice of hydrotherapy and mud baths still flourishes in many parts of Europe, the role of spas as focal points of international diplomacy, the genesis of important works of art, and the spiritual and physical regeneration of their creators is nowadays almost totally extinguished. Yet a glance at the worlds of politics, literature and music during the period encompassed by this essay reveals just how central to the lives of many of its most memorable figures was a visit to a spring or a bath, everywhere on the map of the continent, from Strathpeffer, Llangammarch and Lisdoonvarna in the north and west to points southerly and easterly such as Ischia, Caldas da Rainha and Essentuky.

It was at Plombières that Napoleon III and Camillo Cavour decided on the war with Austria which unified Italy; and from Bad Ems that Bismarck despatched his fateful telegram designed to lure the very same emperor into the Franco-Prussian war. During regular visits to Marienbad, Edward VII, with Admiral Jacky Fisher and the Liberal premier Henry Campbell Bannerman in tow, sought somehow to keep alive the fragile European peace menaced by hyper-militarized imperial Germany. At Baden-Baden meanwhile, Hector Berlioz gave the premiere of *Béatrice et Bénédict*, his operatic version of Shakespeare's *Much Ado About Nothing,* and the poet Jules Laforgue – though he wrote disgustedly of his fellow visitors as 'ces gens stupides et vides' and complained that 'on mange trop bien, on fume trop' – paid no less than eight visits to the spa. Ivan Turgenev, taking the waters here in 1862, was irked at always having to see 'the same faces, all with the same stupid, desperate, rapacious, almost ferocious expressions'. At another German spa, Badenweiler, Anton Chekhov died in 1904, after seeking a last desperate cure for his chronic consumption. Half a century earlier in Homburg – which, like Baden-Baden, combined hydrotherapy with a casino – his fellow Russian Fyodor Dostoevsky had literally lost the shirt off his back at the gaming tables. His novel *The Gambler* is one among scores of books whose plots are partially located amid the intriguingly ambiguous social milieu provided by life in a spa at the height of the season.

That such places had a beneficial effect which transcended the purely physiological was discerned by another writer, Sir Walter Scott, in his *Saint Ronan's Well* (1823), a tale set in an imaginary Scottish watering place. 'The invalid often finds relief from his complaints,' notes the novelist, 'less from the healing virtues of the Spa itself, than because his system of ordinary life undergoes an entire change, in his being removed from whatever else forms the main source of his constant anxiety at home.' Scanning Victorian and Edwardian spa advertising, we may wonder whether this, after all, is not the point. Can Mr C.J. Williams, secretary of the Spa Baths at Woodhall in Lincolnshire, genuinely have believed in the therapies for gout, uterine diseases and rheumatism offered by its Bromo-Iodine Waters and Granular Effervescing Salts (2 shillings per Bottle)? At the Black Forest bath of Freudenstadt, was it the Milk Cure, Terrain Cure and Elevated Air Cure which did the trick? Or, was it – according to the principle enunciated by Scott – the 'Lovely Pine Woods', 'View of the Alps', or 'Music daily'? Could the restorative effects of these pleasures compete with the local sanatorium 'Recommended to Nervous Subjects' run by Dr Lieb? It comes as a distinct shock to find Barèges, high in the Pyrenees, with its 'Sodio-Sulphuretted, chlorinated, alkaline, arsenical waters', advertising treatments for the after-effects of wounds in battle, retention of foreign bodies, infantile paralysis and 'serious syphilis'. The baths at Goerlitz, in the German duchy of Schleswig Holstein, even boasted a re-education programme for young nervous patients – 'Moral weakness and bad habits corrected'.

The *embarras de choix* among the various waters was astounding. In a popular specialized guidebook, *The Health Resorts of Europe*, which had reached its tenth edition by 1902, the American doctor Thomas Linn, based at Nice and Aix-les-Bains, lists nearly a hundred baths, with details of their climate, therapeutics, medical staff, hotels and seasonal dates, together with scientific analyses of the curative springs. In Italy, for example, the saline waters of Montecatini bubble up at 90 degrees Fahrenheit, with a laxative effect which (perhaps surprisingly) invokes their use in cases of dysentery and enlarged spleen. Bormio's geysers bubble still hotter, perfect for 'gouty diathesis' and rheumatism. Casciana di Pisa, with its heavy deposits of lime sulphate and carbonic acid, works wonders with diabetes, anaemia and heart disease.

Yet more seriously engaged than Thomas Linn with the whole issue of what water cures are capable of achieving, both therapeutically and psychosomatically, is the comprehensive survey undertaken in 1898 by Dr Hermann Weber and his wife Frances Parkes, doctors attached to London's German Hospital in Dalston. The former advertises himself as 'Corresponding Member of the Balneological Society of Berlin'. There was, it seems, no comparable organization in Britain, whose spa culture would never attain the sophistication and seriousness implicit in 'balneology'. The fact that my copy of *The Mineral Waters and Health Resorts of Europe* bears library stamps from the Royal Army Medical College and the Ministry of Health, and that both these are overprinted with HM Stationery Office's cancellations, tells its own tale of the completeness with which Britain would turn its back on the entire concept of hydrotherapy as a standard feature of medical treatment.

It was the Great War which appears to have administered the decisive stroke. Not only were many hitherto flourishing British spas turned into convalescent stations and hospitals for wounded service personnel from the various fronts and maritime combat zones. There was, quite possibly, a subtext of patriotic Germanophobia attached to the reluctance of Britons themselves to visit places whose function, layout and architecture were so blatantly linked with the Bavarian, Prussian or Austrian *brunnen* and *quellen* they had been so happy to patronize before the war. Certain thermal establishments on this side of the Channel even boasted a building named 'The Kursaal'. Imitation as the sincerest form of flattery could scarcely get more German than that.

Added to this was doubtless another association altogether – with an Edwardian pre-war world of leisured self-indulgence, whose servant problem was only just starting to loom in many an upper-class or bourgeois household, and where the pace of existence allowed, or even dictated (given the tendency to over-eating), long annual spells of none too penitential inactivity in some Hotel Metropole, Bristol or Angleterre, under the supervision of doctors and masseurs. Though one or two centres, such as Bath and Harrogate, were robust enough to sustain the reputation of their water cures as genuinely effective, hydrotherapy for the British simply fell out of fashion – for ever, it now seems. The gouty and dyspeptic renounced the waters of Askern, Gilsland and Radipole, the colliers of the Rhondda Valley abandoned their annual July trip to Llanwrtyd Wells, the springs of Moffat in Dumfriesshire no longer fortified sufferers from 'slight anaemia and debility', while Ashby-de-la-Zouche, whose saline waters, rich in calcium sulphate and carbonate, were formerly prescribed for scrofula and rheumatism, had to fall back on its fame as the scene of the tournament in *Ivanhoe*.

Whatever happened, meanwhile, to Hermann Weber and Frances Parkes? Was their pet dachshund attacked by angry dowagers wielding umbrellas; did patriotic Dalstonians chuck bricks through the surgery windows; were they resourceful enough to change their name to a more English-sounding 'Webber'; or did they merely cut their losses and retreat to Berlin while the going was good? Their monument, in *The Mineral Waters and Health Resorts of Europe*, is of the *aere perennius* variety for anybody (and this includes the present writer) who actually believes in the therapeutic value of water cures. The map unfurled by that work is of a Europe which is effervescent, positively overflowing with promises of health, longevity, survival or actual rejuvenation, to be fulfilled through the purity and abundance of springs alkaline, chalybeate, arsenical, calcareous, muriated or sulphated. For the patient reader, fascination is enhanced as much by the unrelenting seriousness with which the Webers retail their information, as by their adoption of a specialized vocabulary equivalent, in modern medical terminology, to those vanished languages of Central Asia or the Western Pacific, which ethnologists struggle to reconstruct.

Terms such as 'erethic', 'strumous', 'lardaceous', 'rectal catarrh' or 'malarial cachexia' transport us to a world of wing-collared physicians with Gladstone bags and a pharmacopoeia administered in glass-stoppered brown bottles labelled 'The Mixture' or 'The Tablets'.

In the heyday of the English spa craze, which lasted roughly a hundred years – the exact period, indeed, discussed in this essay – the most resoundingly successful of all native water cures was based, ironically, on the fact that the springs in question possessed no mineral content whatever. As one wag put it,

'Malvern water,' said Doctor Wall,
'Is famed for containing nothing at all.'

The various wells of the Malvern Hills, the great outcrop of pink granite forming a southern frontier between the counties of Worcestershire and Herefordshire, had been famous since the Middle Ages for the relief they apparently afforded to sufferers from skin diseases and eye infections. It was the enterprising eighteenth-century doctor John Wall, already distinguished as the founder of an infirmary and a porcelain factory in the nearby city of Worcester, whose *Experiments and Observations on the Malvern Waters* first popularized the springs for their exceptional softness and purity. Within a year of the book's publication in 1756 the number of visitors to what was then little more than a cluster of village houses gathered around a medieval priory church had trebled, and soon the lower slopes of the hills were scattered with Italianate villas, *cottages ornées*, and essays in the Grecian or the Gothick. In the fullness of time came multiple flourishes of Scotch baronial and French manorial, together with some notable examples of 'the House Beautiful' à la William Morris, and of the Arts and Crafts style which this fathered.

The summit of Malvern's popularity as a water cure coincided with the Victorian cultural apogee in all its restless fecundity. A serious therapeutic regime, pioneered by Doctors Wilson and Gully and based on the ideas of the German homoeopath Vincenz Priessnitz, offered a deliberate alternative to the orthodox medicine of the period, an affair of leeches, emetics, purgatives and black draughts. The new system depended on an availability of adequate exercise, up and down extremely steep hills, a properly regulated diet, and fresh country air. Until at least 1860, Malvern was notable for having almost nothing in the way of urban sprawl: a ten-minute walk from the town led to fields and farms in all directions. Supervised by Wilson and Gully (the latter a perfect martinet when it came to health), patients underwent a three-week course of cold-water treatment in a variety of different forms.

An average day would start at 5 a.m. with a wrapping of the entire body in wet sheets, giving it an oddly mummified appearance. Forbidden anything in the way of breakfast, the willing victim, thus cocooned, spent about an hour on a wooden pallet, before being unwrapped and plunged in a tepid bath. After this came a vigorous massage, then, following the process of drying and dressing, a walk to the nearest well, where they were made to drink at least ten, sometimes as many as eighteen, tumblers of water.

By now, sufficiently hydrated, you were ready for a breakfast of dry toast, boiled rice, milk, water and cold meat. At noon came 'the tonic sitz', in which the patient sat in a cold-water hip-bath to benefit 'the most undignified parts'. This particular treatment was aimed at everything from cystitis, menstrual problems and difficulties in the early stages of pregnancy, to haemorrhoids, obstruction of the bladder and the chronic constipation which so many Victorians endured as a result of over-eating and a generally sedentary lifestyle. An alternative therapy was offered by something called the lamp bath, consisting of a lighted spirit lamp placed under a hollow chair on which the sufferer, enveloped in blankets, sat sweating profusely, dabbed now and then by an attendant with a cold sponge, before being tumbled into a cold plunge and rubbed dry. The whole sequence represented the nearest most English water-cure patients had so far come to the sauna principle adopted a century later from Sweden, Finland, and Russia.

The culminating moment of the Malvern water cure arrived with the douche, which took place in one of the various little cottages erected for the purpose. Having undressed, patients descended to a duckboarded shower room, where an attendant stood ready to pull a chain, 'launching down upon the body a straight, unbroken column of water, one hogshead per minute'. The ritual of 'the falling douche', though it only lasted about five minutes, was sufficiently drastic to be prescribed for just a single session each day, but it was this, more than any other feature of the regime, which seems to have made patients feel that the cure as a whole was well worth the expense.

Practically every Victorian of any note during the nineteenth century's middle decades fetched up at Malvern. The Queen herself, as a mere princess, had visited with her mother the Duchess of Kent and the odiously omnipresent Sir John Conroy. Among the poets, Wordsworth, Tennyson and Swinburne each drank their glassfuls and – at least in the two latter cases – experienced their douches, sitz and lamp baths. Florence Nightingale retreated here after the Crimean War and the hospital horrors of Scutari. Having earlier dismissed the water cure as 'a highly popular amusement among athletic in-valids', she now began a half-century as the nation's most powerfully influential valetudinarian with a sustained course of treatment by Dr Edward Johnson, who had followed Wilson to the town from a less successful spa in Hertfordshire, close to the modern Stansted airport. Repentant of earlier negative judgements, she later claimed that 'I would not be here were it not for Malvern.'

For Charles Darwin, a serious hypochondriac, Malvern offered a significant palliative to the stresses of scientific research. 'I have experienced enough to feel sure,' he declared, 'that the cold water cure is a great and powerful agent and upsetter of all constitutional habits and induces the most complete stagnation of mind.' The term 'stagnation' in this case was used positively, in its sense of passive mental surrender to the more restful aspects of the Malvern cure. Back home at Down House, Darwin devised his own version of the Wilson Gully regime, complete with lamp bath and freezing douche.

Charles Dickens, cynical as he was as to the exaggerated heartiness of 'the cold-waterers' bouncing up and down the granite slopes, recommended the spa to Wilkie Collins. Their friend Edward Bulwer-Lytton grew typically effusive on the subject of wet sheets and cold packing in his Confessions of a Water Patient (1846): 'It seems a positive cruelty to be relieved from this magic girdle in which pain is lulled and fever colled and watchfulness lapped in slumber.' Lytton's little essay may later have been studied by Henry James, who arrived in Malvern on 7 February 1870 for the first of several visits in search of a cure for what his brother William called 'the moving intestinal drama of constipation'. Taking 'the d-d running sitz' among 'such a group of worthy, second-rate Britons as invests with new meaning and illuminates with a supernatural glow the term common-place', the New York writer began here that infinitely ambiguous, hyper-inflected love affair with England which lasted for the rest of his life.

Longing for American vegetables, and bored with a diet of cold mutton and rice pudding, James solaced himself with the beauty of the landscape, 'the immense misty plain of hedges-checkered Worcestershire', and of the sky, 'tremendous and Turneresque, a chaos of rolling grey, a rain of silver, a heaven of distant blue'. On 26 March, however, he received a letter from his parents informing him of the death of Minny Temple, an adored cousin, who, though he probably wasn't in love with her as is sometimes suggested, had become the tutelary spirit of his awakening sensibilities. The loss would leave a permanent scar, its ache renewed many years later in his novel *The Wings of the Dove*.

James was the most fluent, sympathetic and captivating letter writer of the nineteenth century – or of any other, some might say. The correspondence with his family during the Malvern visit of 1870 has its own compelling narrative thread, in which the progress of the cure is interwoven with his growing attachment to England and a simultaneous dislike of a certain kind of Englishness, manifested on this occasion in the almost brutish mediocrity of those around him at the spa. The young Minny Temple's premature death from consumption provides a tragic climax to the whole episode and one whose impact was sharpened by James's physical remoteness from the event itself. 'How strange it is,' he told his mother, 'for me to be pondering her death in the midst of this vast indifferent England which she fancied she would have liked. Perhaps! There was no answering in the whole bright landscape for the loss of her liking.' A few days later, in a letter to William, it was the same Malvern prospect upon which James vented his agonized frustration at the loss of Minny. 'The landscape assents stolidly enough to her death: it would have ministered but scantily to her life. She was a breathing protest against English grossness, English compromises and conventions – a plant of pure American growth.' In only a few years, nevertheless, he would be back again in the land whose likely consolations he now so angrily rejected, writing exuberantly from London: 'I take possession of the old world – I inhale it – I appropriate it!' Malvern, for all its callous indifference to his suffering, had planted a seed whose germination would eventually result in the abundant flowering of his mature novels and stories.

If I've lingered unduly on the subjects of the Malvern water cure and, by association, on one of its most distinguished patrons, it's because, from several aspects, the evolution of nineteenth-century spas like this one goes hand in hand with that of the guidebook, the two presenting complementary facets of an overarching culture of travel. Malvern, not unnaturally, produced its own printed guides. From one such, published in 1862, an entire jostling Victorian world of gadgetry, patent nostrums, social pretensions and shameless publicity jumps out to grab our attention. At Sparkes's Ironmongery we can buy our hip-baths and sitzes, along with meat-hasteners, carpet-bags, perambulators and looking glasses. Lamb's Royal Library & Bazaar will furnish us with 'Cedar Trays & Oak What-nots, Banner Screens for the Chimneypiece, Silver and Plated Fish Knives, Pocket Flasks, Harmoniums and Farina's Eau de Cologne'. James Hill's Homoeopathic Pharmacy, rich in 'Globules, Tinctures, Pilules & Titurations', is also agent for Epps's Chocolate Essence, and in buying our tea at Jones's Family Grocer, we shall have due regard for 'the special attention given in selection of finest growths to suit the splendid water of the Malverns'. T.S. Johnson, a more orthodox chemist than James Hill, offers a dietary supplement called Peptomalt at 7/6d a bottle and 'Mrs Colonel Rigby's Compound Extract of Pomegranate, For Restoring Grey Hair to its Original Colour without

Dyeing'. If, on the other hand, dying rather than dyeing is our Malvernian destiny – and the air of the hills was restorative enough, even in the mid-twentieth century, to buck the standard actuarial trends elsewhere in England – then Horton's Livery Stables will attend our funeral with a shellibier, a kind of undertaker's omnibus to cart the mourners at a suitable decorous pace to the graveyard.

Pausing to consider details such as these while we scan a nineteenth-century guidebook, we engage in an exercise not dissimilar to the archaeologist's, in which everyday objects cast aside or forgotten by more remote generations assume an almost magical significance. Among modern writers there's a fashion for trying to reconstruct the Victorian era by brandishing its impedimenta in the face of the reader, as if the presence of a meat-hastener, an oak what-not or a dash of Mrs Colonel Rigby's Compound Extract of Pomegranate could guarantee an ultimate authenticity. There can be nothing wrong, inherently, with trying to create those literary works we might feel the period should have produced but somehow never did, or with finding a voice, among the various characters involved, for society's disenfranchised or inarticulate representatives. In the case of foreign travel, however, the period's own authors turn out to have covered the ground with a more than adequate thoroughness. At the start of his poem *Red-Cotton Night-Cap Country* (1873), a short novel in verse based on the sensational details of a recent French court case, Robert Browning celebrates the

> Meek, hitherto un-Murrayed bathing-place
> Best loved of sea-coast-nook-ful Normandy

from which his narrative will take its flight. The irony here is obvious. Almost nowhere in western Europe was now un-Murrayed or indeed un-Baedekered, and much of the continent was becoming increasingly familiar to travellers with the spread of national railway networks, while the guidebooks themselves made cities, mountains, rivers, regions or whole countries into objects of suddenly attainable desire.

—

Such accessibility had its impact on the imaginative literature of the period. Early nineteenth-century novelists tended to confine their plots to locations which would be familiar to their readers or at least get-at-able by the more adventurous among them. With the exceptions of *Quentin Durward*, set in Burgundy, and *Anne of Geierstein*, with its Swiss backdrops, all of Sir Walter Scott's narratives unfold in Scotland or England or – as in *Rob Roy* and *The Heart of Midlothian* – a combination of both. Jane Austen's characters, in venturing beyond the comfort zones of the village or the shire, are frequently punished by the writer for their temerity in so doing.

Fanny Price, for example, by abandoning Mansfield Park for a visit to her parents in Portsmouth, implicitly contributes to the implosion of the Bertram family's domestic calm through removing the single moral constant – in the shape of herself – on which it has tended more and more to rely. Emma Woodhouse, travelling only a few miles from Highbury to Box Hill for a picnic, is rewarded with a nemesis devastating enough to demolish the anti-heroine originally intended by her creator, before she is reconstituted on more acceptable moral lines with the help of Mr Knightley, Miss Bates and Harriet Smith.

Emma admits at one point that she has never seen the sea. Austen's older contemporary Anne Radcliffe, author of *The Mysteries of Udolpho*, *The Italian* and *The Romance of the Forest*, herself almost managed not to, but did make a journey down the Rhine with her husband in 1794, the only time she ever went abroad. Her continental settings for these three novels belong to a fantasy world dreamed up from engravings of works by Salvator Rosa and Claude Lorrain in which castles perch on beetling crags, hermits inhabit moss-grown caverns, and gangs of banditti lurk amid shaggy woods and cliffs looming above 'horrid gulphs'. That Radcliffe had no first-hand experience of the Italy and France she so lavishly and painstakingly portrays is a significant reflection of the new aesthetic value-system energizing the Gothic genre in whose development she was such a pioneering figure. Authenticity in this kind of fiction is guaranteed not by hands-on experience but by what another of the period's novelists, the more sceptically inclined Susan Ferrier, calls 'the lurid glow of a romantic imagination'. In the Gothic novel a witnessed actuality is less important than those higher truths manufactured by a fertile fancy.

By the 1830s the situation as regards the capacity and disposition of novelists and poets to travel had changed for ever. The growth of popular fiction in cheap editions and the development of publishing as a profitable enterprise marched in step with the Murray–Baedeker world of mass tourism. An obvious result is the wide range of Victorian writing which accommodates 'abroad' within its purview, whether as background or foreground. Poets of the mid-century began invoking the foreignness of specific locations as an essential element in that transformative emotional experience crystallized by their verses. Arthur Hugh Clough's *Amours de Voyage*, a poetic narrative cast in the form of an epistolary novel set against the backdrop of the Italian Risorgimento, and Matthew Arnold's *Stanzas from the Grande Chartreuse*, a meditation on contrasted lives of action and study with obvious relevance to the poet's own predicament, are outstanding examples of this new enthusiasm: a direct consequence of that sudden ease of movement which the guidebooks were intended both to complement and to advertise.

Some Victorian poets simply wrote about such places for their own sake, or because the journey itself, once completed, kept on tugging at the memory. One of the more unlikely transmogrifiers of travel into verse was Dante Gabriel Rossetti, better known to us as one of the most accomplished English practitioners of the sonnet form, an outstanding translator from the medieval Italian poets and the creator of that mesmerizing synthesis of religion and eroticism, *The Blessed Damozel*. With his friend and fellow Pre-Raphaelite painter William Holman Hunt, he set off for a trip to Paris and Belgium. The pair almost certainly took with them Murray's recently published *Handbook for Belgium and the Rhine*, which contains helpful notes on the principal art works in Bruges, Ghent and Antwerp, while also offering practical advice on making the most of Belgian railways, evidently at a more advanced stage of development than the network in Britain itself.

In a fascinating poetic travelogue, left unfinished, alas, Rossetti attempts to convey the impact of what was probably his first long journey by rail. Successive blank-verse paragraphs try as faithfully and realistically as possible to re-create the alien visual and auditory effects of journeying at speed through a sequence of trackside landscapes: London to Folkestone, Boulogne to Amiens, Antwerp to Ghent. There are sections on a visit to the Morgue in Paris (Browning's poem *Apparent Failure* springs from a comparable experience a few years later) and on the pleasure of arriving in Brussels after

> Toothache, and headache, and the ache of wind
> And huddled sleep, and smarting wakefulness,
> And night, and day, and hunger sick at food,
> And twenty-fold relays, and packages
> To be unlocked, and passports to be found.

This is, so far as I know, the earliest attempt by an English poet of any real quality to engage with the spanking new experience of the railway, frightening and monstrous as it seemed to so many of Rossetti's contemporaries. The journey from London to the English Channel shows a painterly eye for details of movement and space, noting

> A constant sky
> Still with clear trees that let you see the wind,
> And snatches of the engine-smoke, by fits
> Tossed to the wind against the landscape, where
> Rooks stooping heave their wings upon the day.

Not since Wordsworth had a writer sought to render so precisely the impression on the senses made by his surroundings. Once the travellers reach Boulogne and set off for Amiens and Paris in a French train, ancestor, it would seem, of the modern TGV, the sheer thrill of speed kicks in.

> The steam
> Snorts, chafes and bridles, like three hundred
>   horse,
> And flings its dusky mane upon the air.

Dropping in on the Paris Morgue, a must-see for mid-nineteenth-century visitors, Rossetti and Hunt contemplate a murder victim fished out of the Seine.

> Now, very likely, he who did the job
> Was standing among those who stood with us
> To look upon the corpse. You fancy him –
> Smoking an early pipe, and watching, as
> An artist, the effect of his last work.

This whole vivid portfolio of verse sketches ends with a sort of Rossettian homage to Turner, the first great artist to include a train in one of his paintings, as the tourists hurtle towards Ghent under 'the thin swift moon' and the wheels on the track send sparks flying into a tumultuous darkness:

> Now
> Our engine's heat is fiercer, and flings up
> Great glares alongside. Wind and steam and
>   speed
> And clamour and the night.

Fiction, even more than poetry, embraced the imaginative stimulus presented by the world of continental tourism which Murray and Baedeker were busy encapsulating in their scarlet or crimson volumes. Almost every Victorian novelist takes their characters abroad, sometimes for a goodly stretch of the narrative. A single distinguished exception is Thomas Hardy, though at various times during his life he made journeys to France, Switzerland and Italy. Certain characters in his Wessex novels, indeed, are identified as being more sinful and dangerous for the touches of foreignness in their bloodlines. Would Eustacia Vye, for example, in *The Return of the Native*, be a shade less dashingly disreputable if she were not partly descended from a Greek bandmaster, and is Lucetta Farfrae in *The Mayor of Casterbridge* doomed from the outset by being born a Le Sueur from the Channel Islands?

Otherwise the novelists cheerfully pack their traps for the boat train. Dickens, enjoying his jaunts to Italy and France (he lived for a time in Genoa and kept a mistress in a village outside Paris) maps a crucial chapter sequence of *Little Dorrit*, a story which opens on the quayside at Marseilles, according to the phases of a continental tour through Switzerland and on to Venice and Rome. This last location forms the background, in George

Eliot's *Middlemarch*, to Dorothea Brooke's first meeting with Will Ladislaw, and the resultant onset of her disillusion with her desiccated husband, Mr Casaubon. Culture shock in the city of popes and emperors – 'a kind of disease of the retina' induced by the intensity of new aesthetic sensations amid marbles, frescoes and ruins – makes the dawning of this moral crisis the more plausible.

Rome was where Thackeray wrote his delightful spoof fairy tale *The Rose and the Ring*, as a New Year entertainment for his daughters. Earlier, in the guise of a 'Christmas book' in the genre made famous by Dickens, he had produced *The Kickleburys on the Rhine*, a sardonic glance at a party of decidedly average Britons taking the waters and playing the tables at a small German spa. The same milieu provides the background for the climactic final scenes of *Vanity Fair*. It is as an affluent foreign tourist, attended by her dourly constant cavalier Major Dobbin, that the dreary little morsel of laundered virtue Amelia Osborne is confronted by reality in the irrepressibly palpable form of Becky Sharp. Entirely at home amid the more louche manifestations of continental life, Becky is able at last to make Amelia understand that her late husband George, whose death on the field of Waterloo a decade earlier has turned her into the model widow, was in fact a heartless sexual opportunist. Would the scene between these two women, one of Thackeray's most nonchalantly virtuoso performances, have worked quite as well in a London drawing-room? Almost certainly not; the essential impermanence of a hotel, a foreign one at that, affords a more plausible background for the sophisticated irony of Becky's matchmaking. Such it proves to be, since Amelia, having wretchedly abused Dobbin's fidelity to her, is at last driven to accept him through her erstwhile rival's production of the incriminating billet-doux (flourished with a snatch of an aria sung by the scheming Rosina in Rossini's *Il barbiere di Siviglia*) she received from George. Truth, implies Thackeray, or at any rate the truth that honestly matters between women and men, can be better understood in a sleazy, reach-me-down world of German *studentleben*, unmade beds, brandy bottles and half-eaten sausages than amid the hideous self-delusion, hypocrisy, and petty suppressions of the Sedleys and Osbornes back home in London.

The intriguingly ambivalent abroadness of abroad is nowhere better displayed than in the work of Thackeray's fervent admirer Anthony Trollope. This was the most widely travelled of all Victorian novelists. He had climbed Vesuvius and the Pyramids, ridden deep into the Australian bush, lingered in Chicago, Cleveland and Milwaukee, and rafted down remote rivers of Honduras and Costa Rica. Many of his novels and short stories feature foreign settings, Italy in *He Knew He Was Right*, for example, Switzerland in *Can You Forgive Her?*, and Prague in *Nina Balatka* (which draws, incidentally, on details from Murray's *Handbook for Travellers in Southern Germany*, which the writer took with him).

Dedicated as he was to making fiction from the matter-of-fact, that 'complete apprehension of the usual' for which Henry James praised him, Trollope used alien locations and elements of un-Englishness as a means of placing his characters, though not necessarily criticizing them when he did so. Mrs Proudie's disapproving remark in *Framley Parsonage* that 'Lord Dumbello is well known in Homburg and Ems and places of that sort' is a deliberate attempt at disparaging the respectability of the viscount chosen as a husband by the imperturbably glacial Griselda Grantly. Both Homburg and Ems were noted as spas visited more for fashion's sake than for health reasons, and the former's gaming tables were only closed down when the little Hessian principality in which it stood was absorbed by the German empire after 1870, and the management was forced to decamp to Monte Carlo. Griselda trounces the bishop's wife by announcing that she and Lord Dumbello are honeymooning in Rome. Mrs Proudie's daughter Olivia, marrying a mere curate, can only afford a wedding tour to Malvern.

In *Barchester Towers*, an earlier novel in the same series, the Proudies' provincialism is given a salutary jolt by the return from butterfly-hunting on Lake Como of the absentee canon Dr Vesey Stanhope, accompanied by his raffish but distinctly engaging family. The Stanhopes, Trollope tells us, are the sort of people who 'would visit you in your sickness (provided it were not contagious), would bring you oranges, French novels, and the last new bit of scandal, and then hear of your death or your recovery with an equally indifferent composure'. That allusion to 'French novels' is a giveaway – the unnamed prime minister who has recently appointed Dr Proudie to the see of Barchester is shown doing so while 'conning over a Newmarket list' with 'an uncut French novel at his elbow'. The word 'French' is Victorian code for 'sex': thus the Stanhopes are damned before they even set foot in Barchester.

Yet what fun they all are and how Trollope clearly delights in them, ready to jolly up stuffy old Barchester: the doctor who 'had forgiven everything – except inattention to his dinner'; Mrs Stanhope, who never gets up till mid-afternoon – 'The *far niente* of her Italian life had entered into her very soul and brought her to regard a state of inactivity as the only earthly good'; free-thinking Charlotte, subtle corruptor of her entire family; Bertie with his blue eyes and blue suit, dabbling in Judaism, sculpture and 'making love to ladies'; the unforgettable Madeline, a siren Signora on her sofa, perpetual casualty of something nasty, carefully unspecified, done to her by her Italian husband, 'a mere captain in the pope's guard'.

For many who went to live abroad like the Stanhopes, travel became a species of mortgage designed to secure at least a pledge of immortality, and to cater for these a new kind of guidebook sprang up. This was the specialist vade mecum aimed at those with particular reasons to shun the northern climate, a guide which sold the Mediterranean as an extensive sanatorium, a marine spa, rather than a cradle of ancient civilizations. The archetype of such books is Dr Eustace Reynolds-Ball's bestseller *Mediterranean Winter Resorts*, a compact two-part work first published in 1908, reaching seven editions by 1914 and known as 'the invalid's Baedeker'. Reynolds-Ball's priorities are firmly established in his opening chapter on the French Riviera. He devotes five pages to rainfall, mean temperatures, and the drawbacks of the mistral, before analysing the various resorts on the basis of geographical position, sanitary arrangements, and suitability in the treatment of diseases. Hyères, for example, favoured by Queen Victoria, gets a thumbs-up from the doctor for the presence of flushing lavatories in the hotels and the benign effect of its climate on 'brain-workers with feeble physical power' and 'numerous cases of chronic sore throat, especially among clergymen' (Clergyman's Throat was a recognized complaint at the time, like Housemaid's Knee, and is a speciality at several of the spas listed by Dr Linn). At Menton, the drains had been improved following a severe earthquake, but its popularity with consumptive tourists had grown concurrently with an alarming rise in the number of tuberculosis cases among the local inhabitants.

Elsewhere in the Mediterranean, Reynolds-Ball's chief concern, apart from hours of sunshine and adequate sewerage, seems to be the presence or absence of a local English community in which the valetudinarian, with rug, wheelchair and hot-water bottle, can feel properly at home. The organism labelled 'society' in each resort turns out to consist, in Reynolds-Ball's interpretation, of whatever English families or individuals can be scraped together within a five-mile radius. Thus the Balearic Islands, hardly visited during this period by Britons of any sort, are reckoned to have no society at all, but Corfu possesses a few permanent villa residents, a sprinkling of 'literary people' en route to the Levant, and sportsmen off shooting in Albania, whose talk of 'pig, cock, dogs, shooting permits and native beaters' clearly bores the doctor rigid. Tangier looks more fun, though it is 'apt to be resorted to by foreigners anxious to avoid their creditors', and on Capri 'the society is said to be unconventional, and the English and American families residing on the island manage to amuse themselves in a happy Bohemian way'. The era of Norman Douglas's

South Wind or Compton Mackenzie's *Extraordinary Women*, the heyday of Capri as the archetypal sunny place for shady people, is evidently dawning.

At either end of *Mediterranean Winter Resorts*, the commercial supplements are markedly in tone with the ethos of the volume. The heart duly sinks at an advertisement for the Hotel De Belle-Vue at Menton – or Mentone, as we need to Italianize it to be authentically Edwardian – which proclaims among its virtues, besides central heating and electric light, that 'the clientele of the hotel is entirely English'. A positively sinister shudder is induced meanwhile by a terse little notice reading 'All who are affected by super tax or death duties should peruse a pamphlet on the subject by Norwich Union Mutual Life Office'. After all, not many of those forsaking England for the comforts of Nice, Rapallo or Bordighera would ever come back. For some who saw them off from Charing Cross or Victoria, the insurance company's booklet was doubtless indecently comforting in terms of sorting out the less agreeable practicalities of a soon-anticipated inheritance.

Still, the death-marked invalid would almost certainly get as far as Calais or Boulogne with the help of Yanatas, 'The Remedy with the Acrostic Name'. Its letters standing for 'You Are Now Able To Avoid Seasickness', Yanatas carried a recommendation from the late Henry Labouchère, nowadays remembered for his unfortunate clause adding male homosexual intercourse to the list of offences punishable under the Criminal Law Amendment Act. A further testimonial came from the Neues Palais in the German city of Darmstadt, where three members of the princely family of Hesse, who happened also to be the Tsarina Alexandra and the Grand Duchess Serge of Russia (both later assassinated by the Bolsheviks at Ekaterinburg) and their sister Princess Henry of Germany, were each of them happy to sing the praises of the miracle formula in its two-and-ninepenny or four-and-sixpenny bottles.

—

With or without Yanatas, the new Edwardian generation of tourists was growing bolder and more carefree. Baedeker still enjoyed classic status, however, its confidence as a market leader indicated by the fact that nobody in the Leipzig publishing house had seen fit to alter the series's format for nearly seventy years. Just as it had sent the heroines of Henry James efficiently through the Louvre or the Uffizi in the 1880s, now in the 1900s it became a moral touchstone for the characters of E.M. Forster. In *Where Angels Fear to Tread*, the novelist creates an entirely successful pastiche Baedeker entry for the fictional Tuscan town of Monteriano. Mrs Herriton's failure of response as she reads it is meant to damn her in contrast to her son, the ineffectual but sensitive Philip. 'She was not one,' says Forster, 'to detect the hidden charms of Baedeker. Some of the information seemed to her unnecessary, all of it was dull. Whereas Philip could never read the words "The view from the Rocca (small gratuity) is finest at sunset" without a catching at the heart.' In *A Room with a View,* Eleanor Lavish, the preposterous 'lady novelist' who nevertheless grasps accurately the kind of sexual awakening unconsciously desired by the young Lucy Honeychurch, is heard exclaiming, 'I hope we shall soon emancipate you from Baedeker. He does but touch the surface of things. As to the true Italy – he does not even dream of it. The true Italy is only to be found by patient observation.' She confiscates the guidebook and runs off with it, leaving Lucy symbolically defenceless in Santa Croce against an encounter with her destiny in the shape of George Emerson.

Edwardian girls of Lucy's generation might have found more appeal in *The Queen Newspaper Book of Travel,* issued in 1906 by the periodical which later formed the hind legs, as it were, of *Harpers & Queen* magazine. The guide was probably the first ever aimed at a specifically female readership. Facing the title page is an advertisement for 'Mrs E. Adair's Ganesh Preparations', including the Forehead Strap for reducing crow's feet and wrinkles, the Chin Strap, which 'restores lost contours, removes a double chin and keeps the mouth closed during sleep', and a serious-looking box made of japanned tin, containing 'tonic cream, lily lotion, bandelettes, tooth powder and Parisian neige cream'. The magazine's beauty correspondent endorses these products with a nonchalant verbosity: 'More forcibly than ever has the fact been borne in upon me once again that Mrs Adair knows something about complexion treatment that no one else knows.'

With this magic box and a motoring veil and a twelve-and-sixpenny pair of travelling overboots from Abbots of Cheapside, the lady traveller could set off, not just to the Continent but much further afield, according to the *Queen Book*'s recommendations. The guide includes trips to the Victoria Falls, the Seychelles – 'the climate is delicious, and if one can live so far out of the world one will have no reason to repent going there' – and Madagascar – 'Servants cheap and inefficient. Also the moral atmosphere is distinctly unfavourable for children.' In Jamaica, 'the dullness of life in the mountains has to be tried to be believed'. In Celebes, 'the constant wearing of a strip of flannel over the stomach to prevent chills' is advised, while Banjermassin in Dutch Borneo 'has no English colony whatever'. Besides which, the Dutch colonial wives were given to appearing in the local costume of *sarong* and *katabayah*, 'the most unbecoming garment that ever was invented and one in which no English lady would ever appear in public'.

—

What does it all amount to, my poking about amid vagabond clergymen, minor diplomats, down-at-heel Cavaliers, second-rate painters, doctors making a fast buck from gullible patients in the earlier stages of terminal illness, and several generations of British and American tourists with no claim to any kind of distinction? Do the Keating's Powder, the Chlorodyne, the Yanatas, the Izal disinfectant and the McDoddie's vegetables contribute to a larger picture, one which might jostle for the attention of those who demand a suitable degree of Aristotelian high seriousness before deigning to consider the value of these things as the raw material of history? I can't pretend that Baedeker, Murray, their rivals and their imitators demand to be read with the same anxious concentration as that which we devote to *Middlemarch* or *Anna Karenina*, neither of which is clearly 'extra-territorial to history'. I have nevertheless tried, in this short study, to indicate how we might begin to engage with them, in a mood of suitably humble receptivity, as valid witnesses to the century in which those novels were written. Their worth is greater than mere quaint entertainment, though God knows they are amusing in the truest and broadest sense that term will bear – and some at least of their capacity to amuse is consciously exercised. Their integrity of purpose deserves respect. It is possible – and fun, for goodness' sake – to trot a Baedeker around a city, a cathedral or a picture gallery, noting just how much is still there and how much more the anonymous author of 1870 or 1890 manages to tell you about it than most modern guides. Their style – urbane, vivacious, sly or sardonic – is frankly better than most of us tourists deserve. They are, as I have tried to show, creative achievements, not simply an insensate battering of the consciousness with salvoes of unsorted facts. They are my comfort food, my medicine for the hard hours of sleeplessness. To drag in Jane Austen once more, they are my equivalent of Sir Walter Elliot's copy of the peerage in *Persuasion*, which offered him 'occupation for an idle hour and consolation in a distressed one'. Like Sir Walter's, my faculties are 'aroused into admiration and respect', but in this case it is for the selfless energy and dedication shown by the writers, editors and translators of these books. If, like the Kellynch baronet, I feel 'any unwelcome sensations . . . changing naturally into pity and contempt', then these must be for those who can honestly find no species of enchantment in Baedeker's reassuring bulk or in Murray's inimitable mixture of the vagabond, the boulevardier and the virtuoso.

Even an index in one of these books can deliver its rewards. At some time during the 1890s

Murray's indexes changed their format and began absorbing the basic practical information which formerly preceded the historical and architectural accounts of the various cities, towns and villages visited along a particular route. When we take up the *Asia Minor* handbook for 1903 and turn to 'S' for Smyrna, our eyes may start to mist over a little. This is one of several places credited with the birth of Homer, founded at the same time as Troy, mentioned in Herodotus, visited or not visited by St Paul (depending on whom you believe), and home to a venerable English merchant community dating back to the days of Queen Elizabeth. From these nine columns of Murray's index the lost civilization of a great Mediterranean emporium effortlessly reconstitutes itself. There are 62,000 Greeks here, 12,000 Armenians, and 23,000 Jews, most of them Ladino-speaking descendants of those exiled from Spain and Portugal in the sixteenth century. Frenchmen, Italians and Germans run the hotels, Britons provide the coal for the steamers which will take us to Marseilles, Genoa, Alexandria or Trieste. There is a gasworks, an ice manufactory, a Greek hairdresser's, an English girls' school; there are Turkish cafés with raki and narghiles, three casinos, a sporting club, a branch of Savory & Moore's pharmacy, a Scotch Presbyterian mission and an Italian shoe-shop. The latest Parisian boulevard successes play at the Théatre des Quais, where an opera company from Milan presents an annual lyric season. Should we crave anything more exotic, the index lists 'Dancing Dervishes after prayer at the Tekkeh in the upper Turkish town' and 'Howling Dervishes every Friday in the Armenian town'. There's something unavoidably prosaic in that 'every Friday', but it guarantees continuity in the whole polyglot panorama.

An illusion, alas! 'Ichabod – the glory is departed' has since been scrawled across all these nine columns on pages 411–12 of Murray's *Asia Minor*. In 1922 Smyrna, that inimitable conflux of peoples, languages, religions and customs, fell a victim to the cancerous growth of nationalism among Greeks and Turks in the wake of the Great War, and four-fifths of the city was consumed by fire. What has replaced it, in the shape of modern Izmir, is simply a point at which we change boats or buses on the way to somewhere more interesting. Do the dervishes still howl there on Friday? Somehow I fancy not, and even if they do, the experience is worth nothing without the exuberance of cultural contrasts which gave Smyrna, along with the other great Ottoman port cities, Istanbul, Alexandria, Beirut and Salonika, their uniqueness.

Nostalgia is rather a low-rent emotion. It has a sort of bijou heritage quality of which I am normally wary, but in the case of my guidebook collection, such a feeling is unavoidable. It's impossible not to comprehend the vastness of the difference in the world of travel before 1914 conveyed by these volumes, and still more difficult not to experience a frisson, however vulgar and banal, of 'Oh that we were there!' Yes, frankly, with a little money – in 1906 a first-class rail ticket to Vienna cost £7 5s 9d, to Carlsbad £5 3s 6d, to Trieste £8 7s 10d – and with a touch of Keatings' Powder and a spoonful or two of Yanatas, I could cheerfully have sat through a sermon from the boring clergyman at the Mentone hotel church service, and tied the flannel comforter over my recalcitrant liver with a good will. But then that unutterable bunch of spoilsports Willy Germany, Nicky Russia and Franz Josef, 'the dear old Emperor' as King George V called him, decided to wreck it all for ever.

Let me end, in this connection, with a visit to a town in south-eastern Europe, in the company of a 1912 Baedeker. It is 1,762 feet above sea level, it has 26,268 inhabitants, including 15,000 Mohammedans, 2,600 Jews and a garrison of 3,000 Austrian troops. Our passports will be asked for at the hotels, to which we shall have taken the tram from the station. The Grand and the Europa are the best, but the Radetzky is 'well spoken of, with frequented beer garden'. We can call on the British Consul, H.B. Freeman, and have our photographs taken at Konigsberger's studio in Franz-Josefstrasse. There is not much else to do beyond looking at a few old mosques, but we may like to visit Kabiljo's shop to buy attar of roses as a souvenir, and an estabishment in the Appelkai sells carpets and inlaid metalwork. Coming out of this same shop on the Appelkai two years later on a June afternoon, we notice a car suddenly halt and start to turn, because its driver has mistaken the route. Its two most important passengers are a tall, cross-looking military type with a moustache, and an ageing but still attractive woman with a kindly face. As the vehicle begins to back, a man standing on the corner draws a revolver from his coat, and in the echo of the shots he fires we hear the portable paradise of Baedeker and Murray vanishing into air. The name of this town, it hardly needs saying, is Sarajevo.

— Acknowledgements —

When I was invited in 1973, by my friend Christopher Rowe, to address the Norwich School Literary Society, I chose Victorian guidebooks as my theme – not, I soon realized, an appropriate topic with which to engage a group of A-level students. I was grateful for the opportunity to return to it, in an entirely different form and with a more suitable audience, at the Royal Geographical Society in 2005, for the London Library's annual lecture, entitled 'The Portable Paradise: Murray, Baedeker, and the Victorian Guidebook'.

The present work enlarges the discourse still further, while retaining most, if not all, of the 2005 lecture. My thanks are due to Lucasta Miller, a patient and imaginative editor, to Mrs G. Fallows, to the Librarian and Trustees of the London Library, and to the late Holly Eley, who enabled me to publish a shortened version of *The Portable Paradise* in the *Times Literary Supplement*.